CU00821749

PAUL WATKINS MEDIEVAL STUDIES

ELEANOR OF CASTILE
1290-1990

PAUL WATKINS
MEDIEVAL STUDIES
General Editor: Shaun Tyas
Consultant Editor: David Roffe

This new series is devoted largely to facsimile reprints of some of the great classics of medieval scholarship, but also contains important new titles.

1. ANDERSON, ALAN ORR, *Early Sources of Scottish History AD 500-1286*; a new edition with corrections, in 2 vols (1990).

2. HARMER, FLORENCE, *Anglo-Saxon Writs*; a new edition comprising the original work together with her later essay 'A Bromfield and a Coventry Writ of King Edward the Confessor' (1989).

3. STENTON, Sir Frank Merry, *The Early History of the Abbey of Abingdon*; reprinted for the first time since 1913 (1989).

4. SPITTAL, Jeffrey and FIELD, John, *A Reader's Guide to the Place-names of the United Kingdom* (1990).

5. HILL, Sir Francis, *Medieval Lincoln*; reprinted with an introductory essay by Dorothy Owen (1990).

6. PARSONS, David (ed.), *Eleanor of Castile 1290-1990* (1991).

7. COATES, Richard, *The Names of the Channel Islands, a Linguistic History* (1991).

8. FOULDS, Trevor (ed.), *The Thurgarton Cartulary (forthcoming)*.

PAUL WATKINS is also the publisher of the new Harlaxton Symposium proceedings, the first volume of which, on the thirteenth century, will appear in 1991.

ELEANOR OF CASTILE
1290-1990

Essays to Commemorate the 700th Anniversary
of her death: 28 November 1290

Edited by

DAVID PARSONS

STAMFORD
PAUL WATKINS
in association with
University of Leicester Department of Adult Education
1991

© 1991 The Contributors

Published in 1991 by
Paul Watkins
18, Adelaide Street,
Stamford,
Lincolnshire, PE9 2EN

ISBN
Hardback: 1 871615 98 4
Softback: 1 871615 99 2

Photoset from the disks and essays of the authors in Times Roman
and designed by Martin Smith for Paul Watkins (Publishing).
Printed (on long-life paper) and bound by Woolnoughs of Irthlingborough

CONTENTS

5

ILLUSTRATIONS

FOREWORD

Three of the four main essays in this book were first presented at a week-end school at the University Centre in Northampton, which was held in June 1990 by way of a premature celebration of the 700th anniversary of Queen Eleanor's death in November 1290. My Department, which is responsible for Leicester University's public course provision in Northamptonshire, the home of two of the surviving Eleanor crosses, was fortunate to secure the services of my namesake, Professor John Parsons of the Pontifical Institute of Medieval Studies in Toronto, the acknowledged expert in the field of Eleanor studies. It was a happy coincidence that he was planning to visit England around the time of the chosen week-end and that his Institute was both able to release him and to fund his visit. Professor Parsons gave the keynote lecture on the Friday evening to a distinguished audience and set the seal on the whole proceedings. His lead was followed on the Saturday by Dr. Nicola Coldstream and Dr. Phillip Lindley, both specialist art historians of the later medieval period, who are perhaps best known to the public for their contributions to the Age of Chivalry exhibition at the Royal Academy in 1987-88 and to its catalogue. They not only presented the papers now printed here in revised form, but they also conducted on-site seminars around the two crosses at Hardingstone and Geddington (aided and abetted impromptu by Nicola Smith of English Heritage, whose note on the conservation of the Geddington cross is reprinted, with a small change, from the *Conservation Bulletin* by kind permission of the Historic Buildings and Monuments Commission).

It did not seem right that these important contributions should live on only in the memories of those fortunate enough to participate in the Northampton event, and the notion that they should be published developed as the plans for the week-end crystallised. It was fostered and encouraged by my colleague and friend, Professor Charles Phythian-Adams, to whom I am grateful for the suggestion that a fourth essay be solicited, which would put the others into context and which would in particular explore in more general terms the phenomenon of royal funerals in medieval England. The result of his suggestion is the first chapter of this book. I am even more grateful to Dr. Elizabeth Hallam of the Public Record Office for her ready acceptance of my invitation to contribute and her willingness to write at very short notice in an attempt to

7

achieve publication by the actual date of the anniversary. She and her fellow contributors have all been splendid in their efforts to produce text and illustrations quickly during the heat of the summer and between spells of holiday, illness and other commitments. They have also borne nobly my editorial interference. I thank them all.

Two other acknowledgements are called for. Shaun Tyas of Paul Watkins Publishers eagerly responded to my suggestion of co-publication and took on all the production and distribution problems that my Department is not equipped to cope with. He has seen the book through to publication in what must be record time and in my absence abroad on study leave. Finally, like most of the Departmental publications, for which I have recently assumed responsibility, this book has been produced on a nil budget. Despite the authors' having contributed their time and expertise (and their computer disks) free of charge, there have nevertheless been some unavoidable costs, and three of us are grateful to the Francis Coales Charitable Trust for a grant to offset some of the origination costs, particularly that of producing the photographs from which the illustrations have been taken and of copyright and reproduction fees. Some institutions have waived or reduced their fees; to them we are also grateful.

October 1990

David Parsons
Department of Adult Education
University of Leicester

8

INTRODUCTION

The Eleanor Crosses and Royal Burial Customs

Elizabeth M. Hallam

Born in about 1241, Eleanor, daughter of Ferdinand III of Castile and heiress to the county of Ponthieu, was married in 1254 to Edward, son and heir of Henry III of England. Although the match was made for political reasons, Edward and Eleanor's relationship was close; Eleanor travelled with her husband on crusade (1270-74) and between 1264 and 1284 produced eleven children for him. The king's grief on her death in 1290 is widely attested by contemporary and near contemporary sources. One, the author of a St Albans chronicle associated with William Rishanger, drew on earlier material in writing his memorial of the queen some forty years after her death.

While Edward was on his way to Scotland, Queen Eleanor was stricken by a grave illness, of which she died at Harby, near Lincoln on 28 November:

> The king broke his journey, returning with grief to escort the funeral procession to London. For the rest of his days he mourned for her, and offered unceasing prayers on her behalf to our gracious Lord Jesus. He endowed generous grants of alms and celebrations for her in various places around the kingdom. Truly, she was a devout woman, gentle and merciful, a friend to all Englishmen, and indeed a pillar of the realm....
>
> Queen Eleanor's body was taken [from St Albans] to London, where the king was waiting with all the leading nobles and churchmen of the realm, embalmed, and buried in Westminster Abbey with all due respect and honour. Her heart was buried in the choir of the Friars Preachers [Dominicans] of London.
>
> The king gave orders that in every place where her bier had rested, a cross of the finest workmanship should be erected in her memory, so that passers-by might pray for her soul. He also arranged that the queen's portrait should be painted on each cross.[1]

This passage from Rishanger - which was repeated verbatim by the better known chronicler Thomas Walsingham, writing in the 1390s - introduces and well illustrates the major themes of this study of the queen, her reputation, life, death and funerary monuments. Its view of the 'gentle and merciful' Queen Eleanor's character and influence has coloured subsequent historiography and has remained substantially unchallenged until recently. As Professor Parsons points out in his essay on Eleanor's personality and historical context, the Rishanger picture seems to reflect contemporary perceptions of her amongst the poor, but was very much at odds with 'the aristocratic memory of a greedy and vindictive Spaniard who despoiled Englishmen of their lands'.[2] The Eleanor of legend, a model of the devoted wife and virtuous queen, as canonised by Agnes Strickland in her *Lives of the Queens of England*, published in the 1840s, is not the same person who emerges from the close study of relevant contemporary legal and administrative records which Professor Parsons has undertaken.[3] Parsons's Eleanor is a far more believable figure than Strickland's, a lively, vigorous, well-educated woman, who elicited considerable devotion from one of England's most able kings, and who was by the standards of her time a concerned mother. A generous patron of the Dominicans, a discerning sponsor of vernacular literature, she was nevertheless perceived by the English aristocratic and knightly classes as being far more greedy and grasping than a royal consort was expected to be, and as singularly unwilling to control the rapacious and sometimes illegal activities of her own officials.

Apart from its eulogistic tone, the Rishanger quotation is interesting for the emphasis it places on Eleanor of Castile's death, on the king's grief, and on his arrangements for the monuments by which she would be remembered - and still is today. Eleanor's burial rituals and monuments, indeed, mark a high-point in the elaboration of royal obsequies in England, a drawing together and maturing of a number of French as well as English ideas and traditions, some of which had originated several centuries earlier, others far more recently. It is appropriate, therefore, that this book, published to mark the 700th anniversary of Eleanor's death, should give a prominent place to the Eleanor crosses and funerary effigies. The commissioning and design of the crosses are examined by Dr. Coldstream in her article,[4] and in his, Dr. Lindley discusses the surviving figures of the queen which were created to adorn them.[5] Dr. Lindley looks also at the gilt-bronze effigies of Eleanor at Westminster, Blackfriars and Lincoln, and sets all the images within their sculptural context; and both writers place the crosses and tomb effigies within the patterns and practices of royal burial in thirteenth-century England and France.

This introductory essay discusses those funerary practices in a broader context and over a longer time-span, to offer explanations for why Edward, having decided to commemorate his wife in an unprecedentedly lavish way, chose not only to split her remains between three churches, but also to build a great series of crosses - at a time when it was easier than ever before to provide personalised intercession on a wide scale by endowing chantries and chapels at a relatively low cost.[6] The themes here treated are the development and elaboration of royal burial practices in the twelfth and thirteenth centuries, and the intensifying personal and political rivalry between the French and the English kings which linked their funerary rituals and monuments with a conscious enhancement of the cult of kingship and the image of monarchy.

Until the ninth century ecclesiastical custom did not permit lay men and women to be buried inside churches; thereafter, most royal families were interred in some splendour in family groups in crypts or special annexes of churches - such as St-Denis for many of the Carolingian and early Capetian kings of France. That pattern of family mausolea continued as the norm in many parts of Europe, such as Germany and southern Italy, but in England and France royal burial practices became more varied and complex in the twelfth and thirteenth centuries. The many new religious orders offered kings and queens a choice of outlets for their patronage; a royal house would offer special personalised prayers for its founder and his family and would hope to attract further largesse from his descendants. The creation or selection of a monastery as a royal burial church can be seen as monastic patronage of a particularly valuable kind. The religious house would gain a favoured status, since most kings were concerned that their tombs should lie in appropriately honorific surroundings; the personal intercession for the king and his family would focus on their remains and might therefore be seen as having extra efficacy.[7]

In the twelfth and the first part of the thirteenth century, therefore, monks, canons and the communities they served vied with one another to obtain royal bones. Just before his death in 1216, King John asked to be buried in Worcester Cathedral, an instruction which was observed to the letter, to the despondency of the monks of Beaulieu, the Cistercian abbey he had founded in 1204. In 1228 they enlisted the help of Henry III to write to the pope on their behalf, asking for John's body to be transferred to them: he had, they argued, promised to be buried there, and they would be able to intercede for his soul the better if they had his body. Their efforts went unheeded.[8] More dramatic were the events following the death of the Young King, Henry II's crowned heir, at Martel in France in 1183. That violent young man had asked to be entombed at Rouen Cathedral, but as his cortège passed through Le Mans, its citizens seized the body and buried it in their own cathedral. The archbishop and people of Rouen retaliated by threatening to raze the city of Le Mans to the ground unless the corpse was transferred to them. Henry II, when asked to settle this dispute, ruled in favour of Rouen on the grounds that it had been his son's choice.[9] This ecclesiastical enthusiasm to obtain royal remains was to continue throughout the Middle Ages and beyond.

From the early twelfth century most French and English kings took considerable care in selecting or creating their own burial churches. Philip I of France, who died in 1108, chose the abbey of Fleury (St-Benoît-sur-Loire), because, one contemporary explained, at St-Denis, mausoleum of many of his predecessors, he would have been only one king amongst many, whereas at Fleury he could be sure to be the sole object of prayer.[10] Henry I and Stephen founded major unaffiliated Cluniac abbeys as mausolea for themselves and their families, Henry at Reading, and Stephen at Faversham; Faversham's original design, which included a specially enlarged choir, related specifically to its use as a burial-church, although it had to be shortened subsequently through lack of funds.

Louis VII of France founded a Cistercian monastery at Barbeaux, again as a burial church, a pattern later followed by John of England; Berengaria of Navarre, widow of Richard I of England; and Blanche of Castile, widow of Louis VIII of France.[11] Blanche acted as guardian and regent for her son Louis IV of France, and in c.1228 created the Cistercian abbey of Royaumont, which was intended as Louis's burial church until the rebuilding of St-Denis began in the 1230s. The Cistercians had throughout the twelfth century allowed some relaxation of their rules ensuring the simplicity of their buildings, but only to a degree: so lavishly generous was Blanche to Royaumont, that in 1253 the Cistercian General Chapter insisted that much of the ornamentation be removed.[12]

Tension could thus arise between royal families, who wished to create mausolea for themselves in a suitably magnificent style, and the monks, whose asceticism could be seen as giving their prayers a particular efficacy, but whose church design reflected the harshness of their rules. In 1170 Henry II, believing he was on his deathbed, promised his corpse to the priory of Grandmont, the mother-house of a highly ascetic order of which the king was a major patron. According to one contemporary, his barons commented that to chose this obscure and austere priory as a last resting-place would be against the dignity of the realm. When he died in 1189, Henry was therefore laid to rest at Fontevrault, a prestigious and wealthy nunnery near the Loire and with strong links with the king's Angevin forbears - although the choice may have been his barons' rather than his.[13] The king's burial here marks the beginning of a move away from the monastic burial church for the single ruler and his family: the abbey was subsequently to receive the bodies of Richard I, Henry's son; Eleanor of Aquitaine, his mother; Isabella of Angoulême, second wife of his son John; and the heart of Henry III, his grandson. Henry, Richard and Eleanor were all honoured with fine tombs, dating probably from the very early thirteenth century and including part of a group of *gisants* or recumbent effigies produced by the monumental sculptors of the region.[14]

The choice of Fontevrault by Richard and Eleanor marks a return to the idea of a family mausoleum, although its loss to the French in 1203-4, along with the greater part of the Plantagenet dominions, prevented its further development in that role, and allowed Westminster Abbey the opportunity to take its place. Like the monks of St-Denis, the Westminster community worked with skill and persistence to build up the importance of its abbey, associating it with the sacral nature and political importance of the English monarchy. The abbey was the foundation and burial place of Edward the Confessor, whom the monks sought to establish as a tutelary saint of the Plantagenets, in the hope of gaining the valuable patronage that such a link would bring them.

Henry II was sufficiently interested in honouring his forebears' remains to arrange for a ceremonial translation of the Norman dukes at Fécamp. If Gerald of Wales is to be believed, the king also prompted the 'discovery' of the bones of King Arthur by the monks of Glastonbury, which took until 1192 to arrange, three years after the king's death.[15] Encouraged by Abbot Laurence and the Westminster monks, he also went to some lengths to obtain the canonisation of the Confessor from Pope Alexander III in 1161. Nevertheless, it was not until after the loss of most of the English lands in France that Westminster was able to gain the royal patronage it felt it deserved. From 1245 onwards Henry III lavished vast sums of money on the first stages of an elaborate rebuilding of the abbey, which subsequently emerged as the English royal mausoleum and coronation church. Popular support remained lukewarm and after Henry's death building work was suspended, not to resume again until 1376.[16]

In France, Suger, abbot of St-Denis (1136-47) and adviser to Louis VI and Louis VII, reconstructed his abbey church, a French royal mausoleum for the Carolingian and early Capetian dynasties, in magnificent style, and sought to play up the links of the abbey and the French crown with Charlemagne; his monks disseminated popular *chansons de geste* emphasising the same message.[17] In 1165, however, Frederick Barbarossa, Holy Roman Emperor, proclaimed Charlemagne a saint and model for his own kingship and exalted his relics at Aachen, thereby pre-empting French attempts to build up a royal cult around him.[18] And although Louis VI was buried at St-Denis, his successor Louis VII was entombed at his own foundation of Barbeaux. Not until Philip II's death in 1223 did St-Denis resume its role as the French royal mausoleum, and the French monarchy still lacked a tutelary dynastic saint thereafter until the canonisation of Louis IX in 1298.

It was Louis IX of France (1226-70), however, who meanwhile had given St-Denis back its pre-eminent place as the major French royal mausoleum. In 1231 Eudes Clément, abbot of St-Denis, began to reconstruct his church, and succeeded in eliciting the help and advice and perhaps funds from Louis and Blanche of Castile, his mother and regent. Abbot Suger's work was left intact but the rest of the church was torn down and reconstructed in the 'court style' of architecture, which was emerging in northern France in the 1230s and 1240s and was closely identified by contemporaries with the king and his entourage.[19] At St-Denis the crossing of the abbey was transformed into a great ninesquared grid, comparable with the martyrium in an earlier basilica. Louis commissioned a series of magnificent tombs for his ancestors and in 1263-4 placed them in the crossing space, carefully arranged in dynastic sequence. Louis VIII and Philip II were at the centre, and sixteen other Carolingian and early Capetian tombs arranged around them, presenting a striking visual illustration of the *reditus regni ad stirpem Caroli Magni*, the uniting of the Capetian and Carolingian blood and royal traditions in the king's immediate ancestors.[20]

Another French court style building of singular importance was Sainte-Chapelle, a palatine chapel constructed from 1240 to house Louis's relic of the Crown of Thorns, and conceived as a reliquary in stone. With Royaumont Abbey, also constructed in the court style, and St-Denis, it was a clear statement of the majesty, piety, magnificence, traditions and power of the French monarchy.[21]

Henry III, whose wife Eleanor of Provence was the sister of Louis's queen Margaret, was anxious to emulate Louis IX; the patterns of their pious benefactions and almsgiving were very similar, almost certainly by design, since when Henry visited Paris in 1262 the two kings vied with one another in ostentatious acts of piety.[22] Early in his reign, Henry III had promised to be buried in the Temple Church in London,[23] and his shift of interest towards Westminster seemed to have been bound up with his rivalry with Louis. Westminster Abbey echoes many features of the great French court style buildings, in its proportions, in its details and in its uses. It was already the principal coronation church for the Plantagenet kings (a role taken in France by Rheims Cathedral), and when in 1247 the king acquired a relic of holy blood, he installed it in the abbey using a special ceremony which echoed those at the Sainte-Chapelle in 1239 and

1241. Moreover from the 1250s Henry interred several of his children who died in infancy there, and in a will of 1253 stipulated that, notwithstanding his earlier promise to the Templars, he intended to be buried at Westminster. In preparation he had Edward the Confessor translated into a new and magnificent shrine in 1269, and on his death in 1272 was buried in the very tomb from which his patron saint had been removed.[24]

Edward I imitated the panoply of the French monarchy far more consistently and directly. His great - if underfunded - Cistercian abbey at Vale Royal, founded in 1270, was quite probably intended as a copy of Royaumont; and in the 1290s he created St Stephen's Chapel, Westminster, its institutions modelled on those of Sainte-Chapelle and its architecture deriving from the French court style. After Eleanor's death, Edward arranged for the Confessor's chapel to be turned into a large-scale royal mausoleum like that at St-Denis, commissioning a magnificent tomb effigy for his father as well as for his wife.[25]

The king was well aware of the political significance of such gestures. In 1278, shortly after the Welsh had been subjugated, he attended the translation of the bones of King Arthur at Glastonbury, a ceremony designed to show them that their hero was indisputably dead and in no position to rescue them from the English.[26] Moreover in 1283 Edward refounded the Cistercian abbey of Aberconway, the burial place of the Welsh princes and a focus of Welsh loyalties. He replaced it with a royal castle and moved it to a site at Maenan, some three miles away, thereby destroying its earlier associations.[27]

The king had also the example of the great Cistercian monastery of Las Huelgas near Burgos in Spain to draw on; founded in the 1180s by Alfonso VIII of Castile and his wife Eleanor, daughter of Henry II of England, it had become the Castilian royal burial church. Blanche of Castile, queen of France, may well have used it as a model for Royaumont and St-Denis; and Eleanor of Castile's marriage to Edward took place there in 1254. Another parallel was Palermo Cathedral in Sicily - coronation and burial church and metropolitan cathedral of the Hohenstaufen Emperors, Kings of Sicily, in the thirteenth century - which Edward and Eleanor had visited in 1270.[28] Edward's works at Westminster Abbey were therefore quite clearly intended to create an English royal mausoleum and major focus of the cult of kingship, a St-Denis, Sainte-Chapelle and Rheims all rolled into one. In this context, therefore, the tomb of Eleanor of Castile was intended to be symbolic of the power and prestige of the English monarchy.

Eleanor's two other tombs, for her entrails at Lincoln and her heart at Blackfriars, reflect further developments in royal burial practices in England and France. The creation of monastic pantheons for single rulers and their families had heightened monastic expectations of obtaining royal remains, expectations which, as these foundations gradually lost ground to great royal mausolea once again, could be satisfied by a gift of royal hearts or viscera. The advent of daily, as opposed to yearly, masses for souls from 1215, and the resulting foundation of memorial chapels and chantries in ever greater numbers, might seem to have offered kings and queens the opportunity for obtaining personalised intercession on an unprecedented scale, which would satisfy all their needs and aspirations: Edward I made full use of these developments by founding a record number of chantries for Eleanor.[29] But for rulers as much as monks the focusing of prayers on their physical remains seems to have been important - and tombs for royal hearts and entrails allowed that special intercession for dead kings and queens to be widened further.[30]

By 1200 separate heart burials were becoming an accepted custom for kings and great nobles throughout much of Europe. On Richard I's death in 1199 his body went to Fontevrault and his heart to Rouen Cathedral, where a sumptuous silver shrine and a tomb with an effigy of the king were built near the high altar.[31] John left his heart to Croxton Abbey, Henry III his to Fontevrault, and in France, Queen Blanche of Castile, Louis VIII's widow, bequeathed her heart to her own abbey at Maubuisson. Later, Philip IV granted the heart of his father, Philip III (d.1285), to the Black Friars (Dominicans) at Paris, and after his death in 1314 his own heart was to have a magnificent tomb at his great Dominican house of St-Louis at Poissy (founded in 1297), close to the heart tomb of his grandfather, Louis IX.[32] That was despite a papal stigmatization of the division of bodies in 1299, which was subsequently relaxed in favour of the Capetian royal house.[33]

The choice of order, too, is significant: Louis IX and Henry III had both been major patrons of the Dominicans, and in his patterns of religious patronage, Philip IV of France, Edward's major rival, sought deliberately to echo his grandfather's interests. Edward I and Eleanor of Castile made grants to a number of Dominican houses, and their son Edward II was to found a great Dominican house at King's Langley in 1308, where the body of his favourite Piers Gaveston was buried with regal splendour. The siting of Eleanor's heart tomb at Blackfriars, London, was at her own request - the heart of her son, Alfonso, had also been buried here in 1284 - but was also very much part of a wider tradition.[34]

16

Edward's placing of Eleanor's viscera in Lincoln Cathedral also has a European resonance. The separate burial of royal viscera emerged in north-west Europe at about the same time as heart burials, but the ritualisation and ceremonialisation of the practice occurred much later. Evisceration of a royal body after death and the separate burial of the entrails was customary in eleventh-century Germany and known in Southern Italy, but was not adopted in France or England until the twelfth century. Its first appearance was clearly a matter of hygiene: Henry I died in 1135 in the forest of Lyons in Normandy, many days' journey from Reading Abbey, where he had asked to be buried. Contrary winds prevented the cortège from crossing the Channel for several weeks, and the royal body was disembowelled in a vain attempt to arrest decomposition. The viscera were given to an abbey founded by Henry - Sainte-Marie-des-Près near Rouen.[35] The Young King, Richard I, John and Philip II and Louis VIII of France were also eviscerated, but hygiene, followed by habit, seems again to have been the principal motive: one chronicler, Roger of Wendover, even interpreted Richard's grant of his entrails to the abbey of Charroux in Poitou as a sign of obloquy.[36]

Not until the second half of the thirteenth century did royal entrails acquire ritual significance. After the death of Louis IX of France at Tunis in 1270 he was disembowelled and his bones boiled for transporting back to France. His ambitious brother, Charles of Anjou, asked for his heart but received the entrails instead; these he carried off to Monreale in Sicily where he gave them a grandiose burial.[37] A number of members of the Capetian royal house who died during the next few years - including Charles of Anjou himself and Peter of Alençon, a son of Louis IX - were subsequently divided honorifically between three churches in a similar way at their own request; significantly, so too was Eleanor's own half brother, Alfonso X of Castile (died 1284), even though such a division lay outside normal Spanish burial practices. Edward I's grant of Eleanor's viscera to Lincoln Cathedral thus had clear antecedents, and its importance to the king is reflected in the scale and elaboration of her tomb, which equalled that of her body at Westminster Abbey, and was apparently more grandiose even than her heart tomb at Blackfriars.[38]

The ceremony of Eleanor's funeral procession, and the magnificent crosses by which it was to be remembered, stemmed also from these same Anglo-French traditions. By the early thirteenth century royal funerals in England and France had acquired their own ceremonial: in 1183 the Young King was buried in the vestments he had worn at his coronation; and Henry II was carried on an open bier from Chinon to Fontevrault, with his face exposed, clad in his royal garments, and wearing his crown. The custom was continued at the funerals of succeeding English kings and, where kings died suitably close to their burial churches, copied by the French and German kings in the early thirteenth century. In the fourteenth century, the English kings were to be represented by a funerary effigy on the bier, as a focus of ceremony, while in France the dead ruler was carried under a ceremonial canopy and given lengthy and ritualised obsequies which symbolised the transfer of power from one king to the next.[39] The elaborate ceremonies during Eleanor's funeral procession, as at St Albans where her body was set before the high altar of the abbey while the monks conducted an all-night vigil and prayers, were very much within these customs.

The route taken by royal funerary processions, too, came gradually to be remembered in both kingdoms, an idea culminating with the Eleanor crosses. In England, William II was said to have built a cross in the Strand, near London, in memory of his mother, Queen Matilda (d.1083), and more recently, Henry III had erected a cross at Merton, Surrey, to commemorate his cousin William of Warenne, Earl of Surrey (d.1240). In France, the priory of St-Julien-de-la-Croix-du-Roi at Mantes was founded as a stopping-place of the cortège of Philip II of France (d.1223), and a whole series of monumental crosses was laid out at the resting-places of Louis IX's funeral procession as it headed north through France in 1271 on its way back from Tunis. These, the 'montjoies', were almost certainly the model Edward had in mind when commissioning the crosses for Eleanor.[40]

In dividing Eleanor's remains between three magnificent tombs - Westminster Abbey for her body, Lincoln for her viscera, and Blackfriars for her heart - and in creating the crosses in her memory, Edward I therefore drew on and brought together a number of funerary traditions which had developed in France and England over the preceding two centuries. The lavishness of his arrangements, too, marks them out as a conscious exercise in image-making, stemming in large measure from the personal and political rivalries of the English and French monarchies. Above all, though, the tombs and monuments display Edward's grief at the loss of an apparently loved and valued consort. In life Eleanor may not have been widely popular with the English people, but in death the honours paid to her by her husband far outstripped those given to any other medieval English queen.

Notes

[1] 'Willelmi Rishanger Chronica', in H. T. Riley, ed., *Willelmi Rishanger...et quorundam anonymorum chronica et annales...*, Rolls Series, **28**.2 (London, 1865), pp.210, 211 (translation from Elizabeth Hallam, ed., *Chronicles of the Age of Chivalry* (London, 1987), p.132); for the evolution of the St Albans tradition, see Parsons, below, p.42, esp. note 76, p.52. On Eleanor's death see D. Crook, 'The Last Days of Eleanor of Castile: the death of a Queen in Nottinghamshire, November 1290', *Transactions of the Thoroton Society*, forthcoming.

[2] Parsons, below, p.41; M. Prestwich, *Edward I* (London, 1988), pp.123-25.

[3] Parsons, below, pp.29-38.

[4] Coldstream, below, pp.55-67

[5] Lindley, below, pp.69-92.

[6] See below, note 29.

[7] E. M. Hallam, 'Royal Burial and the Cult of Kingship in France and England, 1060-1330', *Journal of Medieval History*, **8** (1982), pp.359-80, esp. p.367.

[8] 'Royal Burial', pp. 364, 377; H. R. Luard, ed., *Annales Monastici*, **1**, Rolls Series, (London, 1864), p.25; P. Chaplais, ed., *Diplomatic Documents Preserved in the Public Record Office*, **1**: *1101-1272* (London, 1964), pp.306-7.

[9] 'Royal Burial', p.363; W. Stubbs, ed., *Gesta Regis Henrici Secundi*, Rolls Series, **1** (London, 1867), pp.301-4.

[10] H. Wacquet, ed., *Suger, vie de Louis VI le Gros* (Paris, 1929), pp.84-85.

[11] 'Royal Burial', pp.369-70; C. N. L. Brooke, 'Princes and Kings as Patrons of Monasteries, Normandy and England', *Il Monachesimo e la Riforma Ecclesiastica, 1049-1122* (La Mendola, 1968), pp.125-44, esp. pp.127-32; E. Martène and A. Durand, eds., *Thesaurus Novus Anecdotorum*, **4** (Paris, 1717), pp.1251-52.

[12] 'Royal Burial', p.370; P. Lauer, 'L'Abbaye de Royaumont', *Bulletin Monumental*, **77** (1908), pp.165-215; A. Erlande-Brandenburg, *Le Roi est Mort* (Geneva, 1975), pp.78, 93.

[13] *Gesta Regis Henrici Secundi*, p.7; E. M. Hallam, 'Henry II as a Founder of Monasteries', *Journal of Ecclesiastical History*, **28** (1977), pp.113-32, esp. pp. 121-122; 'Royal Burial', pp.369, 371.

[14] T. S. R. Boase, 'Fontevrault and the Plantagenets', *Journal of the British Archaeological Association*, 3rd ser., **24** (1971), pp.2-10.

[15] F. Barlow, ed., *Vita Edwardi Regis* (London, 1962), pp.112-33; 'Royal Burial', pp.362, 377.

[16] R. A. Brown, H. M. Colvin and A. Taylor, *A History of the King's Works*, **1**: *The Middle Ages* (London, 1963), pp.130-57, esp. pp.150-1. The English always showed a greater interest in anti-monarchical than in official cults: the supposed remains of the deposed and murdered Edward II, buried in Gloucester Abbey in 1327, became a

major focus for popular devotion and financed a major rebuilding of the church in the fourteenth century: 'Royal Burial', pp. 361-3.

[17] G. M. Spiegel, 'The Cult of St-Denis and the Capetian Kings', *Journal of Medieval History*, 1 (1975), pp.43-70; E. Panofsky, *Abbot Suger on the Abbey of St-Denis*, 2nd edn., ed. G. Panofsky Soergel (Princeton, 1979).

[18] R. Folz, *La Souvenir et la Légende de Charlemagne* (Paris, 1950), pp.177-211.

[19] R. Branner, *St Louis and the Court Style in Gothic Architecture* (London, 1965), pp.30-84.

[20] *Ibid*, p.48; *Le Roi est Mort*, pp.82, 128; G. Spiegel, 'The *reditus regni ad stirpem Caroli Magni*: a new look', *French Historical Studies*, 7 (1971), pp.145-74.

[21] Branner, *St Louis and the Court Style in Gothic Architecture* (London, 1965), pp.56-65; Coldstream, below, p.60.

[22] E. M. Hallam, *Capetian France, 987-1328* (London, 1980), p.205.

[23] W. Dugdale, *Monasticon Anglicanum*, ed. W. J. Caley, H. Ellis and B. Bandinel, **6**.2 (London, 1846), p.818.

[24] *King's Works*, p.479; M. E. Roberts, 'The Relic of the Holy Blood and the Iconography of the Thirteenth-Century North Transept at Westminster Abbey', *England in the Thirteenth Century, Proceedings of the 1984 Harlaxton Symposium*, ed. W. M. Ormrod (Grantham, 1986), pp. 129-42, esp. pp.137-39.

[25] *King's Works*, pp.479-85; Prestwich, *Edward I*, pp.113-14.

[26] A. Gransden, 'The Growth of Glastonbury Traditions and Legends in the Twelfth Century', *Journal of Ecclesiastical History*, **27** (1976), pp.337-58, esp. p.355; F. M. Powicke, *King Henry III and Lord Edward*, 2 (Oxford, 1947), p.724; cf. Prestwich, *Edward I*, pp.120-1.

[27] R. W. Hays, *The History of the Abbey of Aberconway, 1186-1537* (Cardiff, 1963), pp.54-77; G. Williams, *The Welsh Church from Conquest to Reformation* (Cardiff, 1962), pp.24-5, 43.

[28] J. Gonzalez, *El Reino de Castilla en la Epoca de Alfonso VIII*, 1 (Madrid, 1960), pp.532-33; J. Déer, *The Dynastic Porphyry Tombs of the Norman Kings of Sicily* (Cambridge, Mass., 1959), pp.16-23; Prestwich, *Edward I*, pp.73-4.

[29] Brandenburg, pp.100-101; 'La Mort au Moyen Age', *Publications de la Société Savant d'Alsace, Collection Recherches et Documents*, **25** (Strasbourg, 1975), pp.7-10.

[30] C. A. Bradford, *Heart Burial* (London, 1933), esp. pp.38-66; cf. B. Golding, 'Burials and Benefactions: An Aspect of Monastic Patronage in Thirteenth Century England', *England in the Thirteenth Century*, pp.64-75, esp. p.74.

[31] *Le Roi est Mort*, p.31.

[32] 'Royal Burial', pp.365-66; E. M. Hallam, 'Philip the Fair and the Cult of St Louis', *Studies in Church History*, **18** (1982), pp.201-14, esp. p.206.

[33] Papal opposition culminated in the prohibition of the practice by Pope Boniface VIII in 1299 on the grounds that such mutilation was against canon law; behind papal

protests may have lain opposition to Capetian pretensions and the disturbing analogy with the relic cult. But the prohibition was to be relaxed by Benedict XI (1303-4) in favour of Philip IV and his family and proved difficult to enforce thereafter: E. A. R. Brown 'Death and the Human Body in the Later Middle Ages: The Legislation of Boniface VIII on the Division of the Corpse', *Viator*, **12** (1981), pp.221-70.

[34] Lindley, below, p.71.

[35] 'Royal Burial', pp.363-4; Henry of Huntingdon, *Historia Anglorum*, ed. T. Arnold, Rolls Series (London, 1879), pp.256-8.

[36] Roger of Wendover, *Flores Historiarum*, ed. H. G. Hewlett, Rolls Series, 1 (London, 1886), pp.282-4.

[37] *Le Roi est Mort*, pp.30, 94; 'Death and the Body', pp.231-5.

[38] Lindley, below, p72.

[39] *Le Roi est Mort*, pp.12-15.

[40] R. Giesey, *The Royal Funeral Ceremony in Renaissance France* (Geneva, 1960), p.32; *King's Works*, pp.479-85; Coldstream, below, p.60.

21

Eleanor of Castile (1241-1290):
Legend and Reality through Seven Centuries
John Carmi Parsons

In 1925 the historian Hilda Johnstone published, as her contribution to a volume of essays dedicated to T. F. Tout, an article that ostensibly dealt with Archbishop John Pecham's role at the Council of Lambeth in 1281. Miss Johnstone's real purpose, however, was to modify traditional characterizations of the archbishop as a fussy, bothersome prelate reined in by Edward I's sense and determination. The significant aspect of the piece was Miss Johnstone's willingness to question the ways in which historians shape their judgments about historical figures, and her opening words are worth quoting:

> Posterity's selective memory, which of necessity forgets much,
> is a little too apt to single out for retention such facts as are
> in harmony with preconceived ideas. A villain is expected to be
> villainous with a consistency rare in actual life, while a hero's
> failures are kept in stricter subordination to his triumphs than
> would seem natural to himself and his contemporaries.

Johnstone's open-minded approach at first elicited little response among her colleagues; some twenty years later, Vivian Galbraith still lamented the persistence of the Victorian taste for history constructed around 'great', 'weak', or 'evil' kings succeeding each other on the throne, and expressed an 'instinctive distrust of these all-embracing moral verdicts'.[1]

Now any schoolboy worth his Stubbs knows that queens are not history in the way that Kings are History. Statutes and parliaments, chanceries or writs, cease to trouble us when we turn attention from the ruler to his better half; perhaps that is why we willingly do turn our attention. But by the same token, royal ladies are more likely to remain the stuff of romance, of 'all-embracing moral verdicts' shaped by 'selective memory'. This is especially true for queens of a period like the Middle Ages that so easily lends itself to romance, and the woman we remember this November offers one of the clearest possible examples of what can be the result.

Eleanor of Castile has for centuries enjoyed a reputation for wifely devotion and queenly virtue she shares with few other English medieval royal consorts; only Philippa of Hainault and Anne of Bohemia could stand beside her, at least in the manifestations to which we are accustomed.

Eleanor is best known to us from the short account of her life in that bible of Victorian moral judgment, Agnes Strickland's *Lives of the Queens of England*, published in the 1840s amid the renewed respect for the British monarchy that followed Queen Victoria's accession. The *Lives* are the work of an author more literary than scholarly who boasted, rather too often, that her lives of the medieval queens were based upon original evidence. But it does not require the eye of a Regius Professor to see that such is not the case as regards her sketch of Eleanor of Castile. Strickland relies heavily on the antiquarian collectors of the sixteenth to the eighteenth centuries - Stow, Strype, Speed, Carte and Pennant, with William Camden taking pride of place. Apart from the rhyming chroniclers the poetaster Strickland quoted with abandon, the only pre-Reformation historian cited with any frequency is Thomas Walsingham, who wrote a good century after Queen Eleanor died; and any graduate student worth his bursary knows that a chronicle written so long after the fact is unlikely to be altogether trustworthy.[2]

Because of the suspicious distance between Queen Eleanor's own time and even the earliest of the sources upon which Strickland relied most heavily, my aim when beginning my research on Eleanor was to discover what sources existed that were strictly contemporary with her, what those records reveal about her reputation in her own day, and how information about her was handed down during the centuries after her death. I do not propose to recount all the twists and turns the path has taken, each moment of exhilarating discovery and every sickening realization that I had got on the wrong track again. My intent is simply to report what I have been able to substantiate, and to suggest some of the reasons how and why Queen Eleanor's reputation over the centuries has come to diverge so sharply from what the contemporary records and documents reveal about the woman. I say 'diverge sharply' at this point by way of mild warning that much of what I must report may surprise those used to Miss Strickland's honeyed pen.

To establish a chronological frame of reference, it is well to begin with a brief summary of Eleanor of Castile's life, in so far as it can be reconstructed from contemporary chroniclers. Born probably in 1241, daughter of Ferdinand III of Castile and his French second wife Jeanne, heiress to the county of Ponthieu in France, Eleanor was married in November 1254 to Edward, heir of Henry III of England and Eleanor of Provence. Like most medieval royal marriages, Eleanor's was brought about for reasons of policy, in this case to resolve old Castilian claims to the duchy of Aquitaine resurrected by her half-brother, Alphonso X of

Castile. She came to England a year after her wedding but lived in obscurity until after the Barons' Wars, possibly because her first son was born only in 1266. In 1270, Eleanor went with Edward on Crusade, though it is hardly necessary to dismiss as fantasy the legend that she saved his life after an attempted assassination at Acre in 1272. The couple returned to England for their coronation in 1274; thereafter the chroniclers remark the queen only when she appeared with her husband at public ceremonies, or when she produced another child - probably sixteen between 1255 and 1284, though only six survived childhood. The one event that called for special remark was Eleanor's succession to the county of Ponthieu upon her mother's death, in 1279. In May 1286 she again went abroad with the king, to spend three years in Aquitaine. When they returned in August 1289, Eleanor was already seriously ill; she died in November 1290 at Harby, near Lincoln, and was buried with great pomp in Westminster Abbey.[3]

Alone, the chroniclers' testimony offers little to distinguish Eleanor of Castile's life from those of dozens of other medieval queens in England or elsewhere: it is when the chroniclers go beyond events to give opinions about Eleanor that they startle us. A contemporary epitaph in the Dunstable priory annals describes Eleanor as 'a Spaniard by birth, who acquired many splendid manors'. A less neutral reference to Eleanor's craving for fresh lands is found in Walter of Guisborough's chronicle, containing an impudent poem once recited to King Edward by some young squires, critical of the king's policies and the queen's taste for real estate: 'The king would like to get our gold / The queen, our manors fair to hold'. The most direct testimony appears in letters to Queen Eleanor from Archbishop Pecham of Canterbury, sharply rebuking her for profiting from usury - a mortal sin in the eyes of the Church - for obtaining the lands of Christians indebted to Jewish moneylenders, for exactions that reduced her tenants to indigence, and for thus causing what he called 'public outcry and gossip... in every part of England'. Pecham also warned the queen that she was blamed by some for the harshness of the king's rule.[4] Contemporary ideas about Queen Eleanor these, plainly at odds with Strickland, Camden and Walsingham, and they compel us to look further into the thirteenth-century sources, if only to be certain we are still talking about the same woman.

In dealing with this material certain considerations will have to be kept in mind. First is the fact that Eleanor was queen, her actions always likely to attract notice and to be judged according to what was expected of a queen. To recall examples of such expectations concerning Eleanor of

Castile, the criticism of her acquisition of new manors makes it fairly clear that a queen was not supposed to be greedy or grasping, and that Eleanor was blamed for the harshness of Edward's rule implies that a queen was expected to ensure that her husband governed with equity and clemency. Confessors' manuals of the thirteenth century advised spiritual counsellors to urge wives to use all the charms of their sex, even in the bedchamber, to induce husbands to improve their lives and so gain salvation;[5] the medieval coronation service offered the Biblical Esther as a model for the English queen while bishops and popes repeatedly urged royal wives to soften the kings' hearts and correct their rule.[6] Society thus hoped that the queens' example of charity and virtue would ensure justice and mercy: we find townspeople at St Albans in 1275 running after Eleanor's coach loudly crying for her help against the abbot's exactions, and the rolls of Chancery are scattered with pardons and grants by Henry III and Edward I when their wives interceded on behalf of petitioners.[7] The other side of the coin is that if the king ruled vigorously, the queen, usually a foreigner in an island kingdom distrustful of outsiders, was likely to be blamed for his unpopular actions. Medieval society did not willingly accept women in positions of wealth and power when that power depended on a husband whom she might influence to her own ends, and chroniclers' accusations against Eleanor of Provence for swaying Henry III show that a queen suspected of using her leverage in the political arena was held to have betrayed the interests of the realm.[8]

Thus perceptions of the queen's influence and authority were sensitive elements in her reputation. Since the queen usually appeared before the public at moments of elaborate ceremony that linked her with the king and with other centers of power - the Church, for example - people naturally came to think of her as powerful and influential.[9] But this was no more than the illusion of power, for her glory was merely a reflection of the king's might. In earlier centuries, a queen's role as manager of the king's household and treasure gave her effective means to secure power for a young son, if need be, and to protect her position; but administrative developments over the centuries meant that by the thirteenth century, English queens no longer controlled those sources of public authority.[10] Just how insecure a queen's position really could be is shown by the troubled widowhoods of Berengaria of Navarre and Isabella of Angoulême, both of whom lived well into the thirteenth century: an uncertain future faced the childless queen, or one who failed to supply herself with loyal supporters attracted by the patronage and wealth she could offer.[11] In later reigns, Isabella of France learned what could happen to the king's wife when favorites seized power, and Elizabeth

26

Woodville paid a tragic price for the narrowness of the foundations on which her glory rested.

It was therefore necessary that royal wives found other ways of securing their positions with solid sources of revenue and dependable followers, and by creating and sustaining impressions of their power. Attention to the pleas of supplicants like those at St Albans, for example, and diligence in obtaining favors or pardons from the king, were one way for the queen to demonstrate her influence with her husband and win popular sympathy for her generosity of spirit. But the queen's ability to dispense personal patronage depended upon wealth, and for an English queen to amass the needed resources in thirteenth-century England was easier said than done. Eleanor of Aquitaine's disgrace in 1173 marked the beginning of some six decades during which the position of queen-consort went into practical abeyance,[12] for the wives of Richard I and John were virtually invisible to the English and Henry III remained a bachelor until his marriage to Eleanor of Provence in 1236. The first years of their marriage saw the queenship strengthened as the new queen was supplied with income from a succession of rich wardships, and quickly came to preside over a complex and vigorous administration. That the increased scope of the queen's activities caused unfavorable reaction is suggested by protests at the Oxford parliament in 1258 against Eleanor of Provence's efforts to increase her prerogative income.[13] And as we have seen, Eleanor of Castile incurred direct and pointed criticism for her aggressive participation in the land market.

It is in the context of the resurgent and controversial English queenship in the thirteenth century that we must consider Eleanor of Castile's career. The chroniclers give no indication that Eleanor tried to involve herself in the affairs of the realm, but Pecham's warning that she was suspected of inclining Edward to rule harshly poses an obvious conundrum: did she stand decorously in the background seeking no public role, or like Eleanor of Aquitaine was she denied such a role? The evidence suggests Edward never considered a politically active role for his wife, and the extent to which Eleanor of Castile influenced Edward I is correspondingly quite doubtful. The testament Edward made after the attempt on his life in 1272 provides no official capacity for Eleanor and in fact distances her from all sources of power: she was assured her dower, but was denied the regency during the minority of their heir, nor was she to be legal guardian of their children.[14] There is evidence, moreover, that Edward did overrule his wife if her behavior threatened to exceed reasonable bounds: in 1287 Eleanor learned that a manor at Southorpe,

27

near her estates at Torpel and Upton, was to be conveyed to Peterborough Abbey through a collusive transaction that would contravene the statute of mortmain. She went to Edward vehemently demanding that Southorpe be seised into his hands, with the quite probable intent that he should then grant her custody of it; but he refused, saying that he would do nothing contrary to right.[15] Even in the arena of diplomacy Eleanor's part was largely formal, as she received envoys and presented them with gifts usually provided by the king.[16]

But the queen did develop one effective area of activity related to both politics and diplomacy, as she involved herself repeatedly in the marriages of relatives and courtiers. As early as 1260, she arranged a marriage between her cousin Jeanne de Châtelleraut and Edward's uncle Geoffrey de Lusignan to reinforce Edward's alliance with his Poitevin kin; by 1262 she and Edward were using their attendants' marriages to assure loyal support in their households, and as queen Eleanor deployed the marriages of wards of the Crown, granted her by the king, to reward her attendants. She thus helped to extend a network of courtly families who owed her their good fortune, an important consideration since a queen needed to assure herself loyal adherents.[17] When it came to her relatives' marriages, however, Eleanor had to be cautious. Henry III and his wife arranged many English marriages for their foreign relatives, and were widely criticized for disparaging English heiresses by marrying them to alien husbands. When Eleanor of Castile came to England in 1255, the English were fearful that a crowd of her relatives and countrymen would now join the throng of foreigners competing for English wealth,[18] but she seems to have learnt from the example of her parents-in-law, for her relatives' marriages did not draw upon her the condemnation heaped on King Henry and his wife. She was lucky in that some of her maternal relatives already had ties to England, and it was from these French houses that Eleanor chose the relatives she married, while importing few Castilians; and the marriages she arranged were almost always for female cousins not males. Thus there could be no complaints that she was disparaging English heiresses or enriching foreign houses.[19] The queen's care in arranging these marriages suggests that she knew behavior within the royal establishment would affect popular opinion.

But public reaction can rarely be manipulated with consistent success, and though we have some evidence that Queen Eleanor tried to do just that with regard to her estates, she was less successful in manoeuvring the response to this area of her endeavors. Eleanor received no lands upon her marriage, and it was only in April 1264 that Henry III granted her the first of the many manors she came to hold.[20] In a letter written some eighteen months later, around mid-September 1265, Eleanor shows that she has grasped the idea that land means money. The letter informs Eleanor's clerk John de Loundres that King Henry lately granted her the wardship of a manor at Barwick in Somerset; but a short while later he mistakenly re-granted the same wardship to someone else. Eleanor had found that two other manors nearby were going begging and instructed Loundres to approach members of the king's council to obtain one of those for her. The most striking thing about the letter is the stress it lays on avoiding any hint that Eleanor sought the manors out of mere greed: '[Say] that the manor of Barwick that the king gave us. . . has been taken from us, for this will tend to make us seem less covetous. . . Be careful to dispatch this matter, for it will be to our profit; and so suitably procure the affair that they shall not put it down to covetousness.'[21] The discreet approach here again suggests Eleanor's concern lest her actions attract criticism; yet her behavior as queen did exactly that, and we are thus faced with yet another riddle about this woman. Was Eleanor deliberately concealing true motives in September 1265, or did she simply cease to bother herself with public opinion once she became queen?

It is important to view this, the most controversial aspect of Eleanor's career, in the widest possible context. First and foremost, we must turn to the principal reason for the queen's land acquisitions, her financial needs. By custom, the king met all his wife's housekeeping expenses when she was living at court: he paid for her food and that of her household, as well as her servants' wages, and only when the queen left court did she pay these expenses from her own coffers. The king also provided money for clothing and shoes for his wife's servants, for her almsgiving while she was travelling and for such miscellaneous items as the cushions in her chamber. The queen paid for her own jewels and clothing, private gifts and personal almsgiving.[22] What we must bear in mind is that if the queen outlived her husband, she went permanently out of court and thereafter had to meet all her expenses. Now Eleanor of Castile's entourage in the last year of her life already included upwards of some 150 people,[23] and since a queen-dowager had a natural obligation to retain those who served her as consort, Eleanor's expenses had she survived Edward would have been considerable. Apart from household expenses, of course, were the costs of maintaining royal state and meeting expectations of patronage and largesse, always serious matters for a queen and often critical for a royal widow.

29

The revenues on which the queen existed came from two principal sources: prerogative income and the issues of her lands. 'Prerogative income' refers to any money that came to the queen because she was queen, for example queen-gold which arose from the operations of the courts of law. Some prerogative revenue came to her through the king's grants, as for example the goods and chattels of Jews condemned for clipping the coin, granted to Eleanor of Castile in 1286. But the queen lost her claim to prerogative income upon her husband's death; a widowed queen therefore had to survive on the second source of revenue, the issues of lands assigned her in dower, augmented by whatever lands she was able to add to her dower. In 1275, Eleanor of Castile was guaranteed dower lands worth £4500, but it is doubtful that this sum would have sufficed for her maintenance had she been widowed in 1290, when an estimate of her total expenses including those borne by the king would reach well above £8000.[24] Half the lands in her dower assignment, moreover, were in Gascony and it was to be expected that there would be problems in collecting revenue from so distant a source. Significantly, the English lands Eleanor of Castile acquired by 1290 were worth around £2600 yearly,[25] roughly equivalent to the value of her dower lands in Gascony. If Eleanor had strong arguments for adding to her estates, then, the king had equally valid grounds for encouraging or helping her to do so. At Henry III's death, his widow entered dower lands worth £4000, half in England and half in Gascony; had Edward died leaving both his mother and a widow, his successor's resources would have been burdened with supporting two dowagers to the tune of some £4200 in England.[26] We can understand, then, why the impressive list of Queen Eleanor's new manors drawn up in 1281 states that Edward helped pay for many of these estates and that the king retained these manors to him and his heirs.[27]

The queen's transactions in fact show repeatedly that the king was her active and approving partner, especially in the highly contentious area of her relations with Jewish moneylenders. As the queen's connections with the Jewry account for much of the scholarly attention paid her in recent decades, it is well to examine this matter before we consider the role the usurers played in her land gathering. In Castile, Eleanor must have associated freely with members of the Jewish faith, who honorably served the Castilian royal family in positions of responsibility and intimacy. The Castilian kings regularly entrusted their financial administration to Jews,[28] and between 1268 and 1272 Eleanor appears to have nominated Jews to the custodianship of the gold due her as wife of the lord of Ireland.[29] Eleanor of Castile's profitable relations with the

Jewry have been contrasted with the fact that in 1275 Edward granted his mother's request that no Jew should dwell in the towns she held in dower, and historians have been led to state repeatedly that Edward's wife was more favorably inclined towards the Jews than was his mother.[30] Certainly a small group of Jews were repeatedly involved in Queen Eleanor's land transactions, and at least one of these men benefited from her patronage when she induced Edward to order his admission as chief rabbi at London, in 1281.[31] But it is not clear that Eleanor of Castile showed more favor towards the Jews than her mother-in-law; there is just as much reason to describe the queen's relations with the English Jewry as calculating, grasping and opportunistic.[32]

At law, debts owed the Jews were on the same footing as any debt and were hence treated as chattels, save that the Jewry's special relationship to the Crown meant that such debts legally were the king's. Before 1269 anyone in England could purchase from a Jewish creditor the debts owed by a Christian, and in the twelfth and thirteenth centuries secular magnates, ambitious clerks and even Christian religious houses secured much land and money by trafficking in these debts. In 1269, however, this practice was forbidden by statute and thereafter there were only two ways debts to the Jewry could come to Christian hands.[33] One was exclusive to the queen: queen-gold was automatically levied whenever the king tallaged the Jewry, and to meet that obligation individual Jews gave the queen an equivalent sum in debts owed them. The other means was for the king either to grant the debts directly to an individual or to sell his licence for their acquisition; and Eleanor was often granted all the debts owed to a certain Jew, or all debts owed by a certain Christian.[34] Once such debts were in Eleanor's hands her demand for payment, or her offer to pardon the debt, often resulted in the release to her of the lands pledged to secure the loan, and it was for this reason that Archbishop Pecham scolded Eleanor for profiting from usury. In practice Eleanor was careful to see that the Christian debtor did receive compensation: the lands might be conveyed to her only in reversion with the tenant retaining them for life, or if she took the lands at once she would assign the tenant for life other lands to the same value. In some cases money did change hands, though not necessarily as much as the land was worth.[35] But it must be kept in mind that the queen would not have obtained these debts without her husband's active cooperation.

Archbishop Pecham's letter with its reference to scandal and rumor caused by the queen's actions, together with the Dunstable epitaph and the Guisborough poem, leave no doubt that Eleanor's landgathering was the most prominent and controversial part of her reputation. The reaction to her participation in the land market can be paralleled with the complaints aroused by Eleanor of Provence's efforts to increase her revenues from queen-gold. This was an irregular source of income that depended on the variable number of voluntary fines levied with the king: hence Eleanor of Provence's efforts to expand the range of fines that produced queen-gold. A related factor in Eleanor of Provence's financial system was that most of the lands she held during Henry III's lifetime were assigned her only in wardship; when an heir came of age and the queen gave up the lands, there was no guarantee of immediate replacement, and Henry often had to supply his wife with cash from his wardrobe. In contrast, Eleanor of Castile held the bulk of her lands on a permanent basis, and her revenues were thus regular and dependable. The unique legal position enjoyed by the king's wife allowed her to control her own property,[36] but Eleanor of Castile participated in the land market on a scale unheard-of for an English queen and her energy plainly took the English by surprise. Queens were not supposed to appear greedy, and as in Eleanor of Provence's case, adverse reaction was likely.

My catalogue of Queen Eleanor's estates, including her dower assignment, the lands held by the king's grant and those added in other ways, runs to more than 250 entries. Obviously I cannot hope to discuss all her transactions in detail, but I will discuss the fine points of one case which offers a number of aspects for comparison with others among Eleanor's transactions. Hubert de Burgh's grandson John de Burgh was indebted to the Jewry for more than £400; the king granted these debts to the queen in the autumn of 1275, and to acquit them John released to Eleanor in the spring of 1278 his manor at Burgh, next Aylsham, which Henry III granted Eleanor in 1269. Burgh was worth £30 yearly, and as in Queen Eleanor's time land changed hands for ten times its extended value, we would expect that John received £300; but because she pardoned £400 of the debts he now owed her the queen paid him only £66 13s. 4d.[37] Now most of John's inheritance came not from his grandfather but from his mother, and Sir Frank Powicke plausibly theorized that John alienated most of his paternal estates to clear his inherited burden of debt.[38] He had in fact surrendered a large portion of them to the king in 1273, and in October 1275 those lands were included in Queen Eleanor's dower assignment. The lands surrendered in 1273 included Cawston, near Burgh in Norfolk, so that Eleanor's acquisition of Burgh in May 1278 formed, with Aylsham, a coherent group of manors in Norfolk, a group the king in fact brought into being in that same month by allowing Eleanor to hold Cawston during his lifetime. Within a few months thereafter, the queen

32

secured a fourth manor nearby at Scottow, through Bartholomew de Redham's debts to the Jewry.[39]

The Burgh case reveals several important patterns and ramifications. First is the relationship between lands included in her dower assignment and lands that she acquired, for most of the estates conveyed to Eleanor were located near manors she could expect to hold in dower. Since widely scattered estates were harder to manage, administrative convenience and efficiency were probably central factors here and that realization throws into relief a second guideline apparent in Eleanor's purchases: the desire to increase the queen's demesne within her manors, an aim not always pursued according to the letter of the law. Though she did purchase other lands at Burgh, for example, her bailiffs at Scottow seized some forty acres as allegedly appurtenant to the manor acquired by the queen; the rightful tenants recovered the land only in 1301.[40] A similar case involved the lands of Henry de Newburgh, who in 1276 sold the queen a manor at Hurcott and other lands in Somerset and Dorset extended at 6 knights' fees; by 1281 her bailiffs there seized further lands extended at more than 7 fees, claiming they were included in the original transaction. Newburgh's son recovered only part of these lands as late as 1305.[41]

The coincidence in time between the grant of John de Burgh's debts in November 1275, and the issuing of Eleanor's dower assignment that October, opens up a network of connections to her other transactions. The Burgh debts were not the only ones granted her at that time; she also received the debts of Robert de Crevequer, lord of Chatham in Kent, and of William de Leyburn who held Leeds castle, formerly part of the Chatham barony that had been sold by Robert de Crevequer's father. Queen Eleanor secured Leeds and Chatham from these men in the spring of 1278,[42] at the same moment she acquired Burgh by reason of John de Burgh's debts. That these Kentish estates were no mere coincidence seems proved by Eleanor's purchase later in 1278 of manors at West Farleigh and Teston, also members of the Chatham barony sold off by earlier Crevequers.[43] Eleanor thus reassembled at one blow a fragmented barony that became the nucleus for the extensive lands she ultimately acquired in Kent - just as John de Burgh's lands in Norfolk were the core of the interests she built up in that county. The Crevequer, Leyburn and Burgh debts, among others, cannot in fact be taken as separate from Eleanor's dower assignment: there can hardly be any question that the lands to be secured through those debts were always intended to supplement the assignment in such a way as to avoid further pressure on the king's lands. The wholesale inclusion in the dower assignment of the lands surrendered by John de Burgh also points to the conclusion that Edward's aim was to provide for his wife without diminishing the Crown's estates.

Eleanor's land purchases did not come about in a vacuum: they are properly seen as an extension of the king's purchases and hence partook of the same 'devious and grasping' nature recently ascribed to those acquisitions by Dr Michael Prestwich.[44] Of course, Queen Eleanor's contemporaries did not have the advantage of all the documentation we can bring to bear on these matters; the king's involvement was presumably not as evident to them as it is to us. Thus it was the queen's reputation that suffered, and the persistence of such opinions can be judged from a 1341 claim in the king's court by the heirs of Robert de Camville, who sought to recover his manor at Westerham in Kent. According to the heirs' version of events, Queen Eleanor once offered to buy Westerham but Camville replied that he had settled it on a son and daughter-in-law. The furious queen then connived with the marshal of the king's army during the Welsh war and made it appear that Camville failed to perform the military service he owed. He was imprisoned until he conveyed Westerham to the queen, and within nine months he died.[45] This strange tale in no way fits the evidence - Camville conveyed his lands to the queen in 1280 because of his debts to the Jewry, and he lived until 1286[46] - but we are less concerned with its truth or fiction than with the facts that it was made after a lapse of sixty years, and that it was only one of many attempts in the fourteenth century to recover manors conveyed to Queen Eleanor. Thomas Tregoz sought to recover Drayton in Sussex in 1321; in 1323 and 1332 Margerie le Lou attempted to recover lands of her inheritance at Grafton in Warwickshire, in the 1330s Gilbert Pecche of Bourn and the Bohuns of Midhurst were seeking lands or rights in Essex and Buckinghamshire, Quarr Abbey sought Whitfield in the Isle of Wight between 1333 and 1341, and Faversham Abbey sued for the advowson of Tring in 1337.[47] The details of all these claims are not known and it is uncertain whether similarly fanciful tales were being told. But that these claims were made indicates that in some quarters during the half-century after her death, Queen Eleanor's virtue and generosity were not necessarily the qualities that sprang to mind if her name was mentioned.

If the evidence proves that King Edward was really behind his wife's acquisition of new estates, we cannot so easily excuse the behavior of the administrators for whom Eleanor herself bore responsibility. These were the men who carried out the unattractive actions associated with the queen, and since the estates entrusted to their care were scattered throughout England their behavior was exposed to popular scrutiny on a wide scale. The effect on Queen Eleanor's reputation is easy to guess, but there is still the question of true responsibility: were the officials merely following her orders? The queen's manorial accounts give no details of the bailiffs' activities, though her wardrobe accounts indicate that she kept in close touch with her officials by messenger, and her constant travels around England brought her to most of her manors on a fairly regular basis.[48] Such evidence, however, permits no more than the assumption that she had some knowledge of what was being done.

But there were public complaints against the behavior of the queen's bailiffs during her lifetime, and these prove that while her officials' arrogant misbehavior was known to her, little was done to correct matters. From 1264 John de Hegham, her bailiff at Ashford, denied the prior of Newstead common of pasture and the prior could not keep his animals there until 1280. Though Eleanor held Barwick for no more than three weeks in 1265, her men seized the Michaelmas rent and the relief due from a tenant of the manor. The bailiffs at Market Harborough compelled the men of Northampton to pay customs and tolls they had never before rendered. At Macclesfield, the bailiffs used the forest as they pleased and mowed the meadows to feed the queen's animals, to the detriment of the game. In 1274 the officials at Harborough were said to ascribe to themselves 'royal right in all things', and in 1280 tenants of the see of Canterbury were distrained to offer suit in the queen's court at Leeds. The bailiffs in the New Forest, summoned to an inquest taken by the king's coroner in 1287, refused to appear. View of frankpledge at Thurgarton and Walton was withheld from the abbot of St Benet Hulme, and suit of court and a money rent from Torpel were detained from Peterborough Abbey. The prioress of Amesbury - where the queen-mother retired and the queen's daughter Mary lived! - had to petition in parliament in 1290 for a rent detained by Eleanor's bailiffs at Woodrow, and for a decision that the priory's men should not be distrained by the queen's steward of the New Forest to pay cheminage or to offer suit of court. In 1290 the king himself remarked that Eleanor's steward Hugh de Cressingham was ignoring royal mandates and behaving in 'unprecedented fashion'. Such behavior was characteristic, too, of the bailiffs on Eleanor's estates in Ireland and Gascony. A stab at setting matters right was made in 1285, when the queen's steward William de St Clare was commissioned to enquire into injuries and extortions by her bailiffs,[49] though this seems like sending the fox to guard the hens and, in the end, it was only the queen's dying wish that opened up her administration to close scrutiny.

Our most comprehensive view of the queen's administration comes from the inquest of 1291, commissioned by the king in keeping with Eleanor's deathbed request that any wrongs committed by her or in her name should be searched out and set right.[50] By its nature this evidence is largely negative, but even so it unmistakably strengthens the impression left by the material already cited. Services and rents were commonly withheld from lords of whom the queen's lands were held, or were compelled from others who did not owe them; lands or rights claimed as appurtenant to estates Eleanor already held were usurped to her use. The auditor, John de Lovetot, helped by drawing up the extents taken of manors acquired by the queen and recording at the stewards' mandate inflated amounts for rents and services tenants owed; the bailiffs then exacted the increased dues from the tenants.[51] The rolls identify the worst culprits: the steward Walter de Kancia and two bailiffs, Robert de Bures at Overton in Flintshire and John de Ponte in Kent and Norfolk.[52] The queen's officials widely abused their positions to their own profit: Lovetot was accused of stealing horses, Ponte of imprisoning a man in Norwich so that he, a clerk, could spend the night with a prostitute in the man's house. Thomas le Taverner compelled the men of Bangor-on-Dee to give him half their catch of fish. Kancia was convicted in the 1270s of massive poaching in the New Forest (where he was responsible for the queen's game) and of openly suborning jurors; he also impeded execution of the testament of a tenant in the Forest, making it appear that the man died intestate and seizing his goods worth £35 10s., which Kancia kept for himself even though he claimed to be acting in the queen's name.[53]

There is no denying that Eleanor's administration was as plagued with venality as any modern bureaucracy. There were, of course, onerous demands on the queen's purse, and her bailiffs were probably given to understand that the production of revenue was their main object. They were, furthermore, exempt from prosecution for actions committed on the queen's service until her deathbed wish exposed them to investigation,[54] and the combination of heavy responsibility and legal immunity could well have gone to their collective head. We must also ask whether the queen's administration was any worse than that of her mother-in-law, which was subjected in 1290 to an investigation whose records unfortunately do not survive.[55] Undoubtedly the behavior of the queen's officials would have attracted attention, and popular reaction can hardly have been positive. But there remains the unavoidable question of the queen's personal role, and here the inquest rolls of 1291 prove that Eleanor was capable of behavior so unattractive that care seems to have been taken to keep the matter quiet.

36

Richard de Stokepord, lord of Stockport next the queen's manor at Macclesfield, once presented Walter de Kancia to the church of Stockport. The queen apparently formed the idea that she thereby acquired some proprietary interest in that church, and when Kancia died she required Stokepord to replace him with another of her clerks, John de Caen. By the time that message reached him, however, Stokepord had already presented someone else and could not comply with Eleanor's demand. The queen then wilfully ordered her bailiff at Macclesfield to torment Stokepord until he obeyed her wishes, so for seven years Richard was distrained, wrongfully impleaded, amerced for twenty marks and otherwise abused until the queen's death brought opportunity for redress. After Stokepord brought his complaint before the justices, the bailiff was summoned into court but was allowed, or required, to give evidence in secret. He acknowledged the truth of Stokepord's claim and admitted that he had acted at Eleanor's orders. Apparently to force the matter back into the open, Stokepord then asserted that the bishop of Bath, the king's chancellor and one of Eleanor's executors, also knew the truth of the matter; obviously glad to rid themselves of the business, the justices thereupon instructed Stokepord to pursue his complaint before the executors.[56]

Stokepord's experience was not unique. We have a letter sent in 1283 by Bishop Godfrey Giffard of Worcester to the prior of Boxley, who was unable to fulfil the queen's request that he present one of her chaplains to a benefice. The queen had written to Giffard about the presentation she desired, and the bishop warned the prior that the royal anger was not lightly incurred.[57] Now the queen had to provide suitably for her clerks, but she controlled a limited number of advowsons and 'inducing' others to present her clerks to their churches was to some extent a necessity for her. Even so, it is impossible to explain away Archbishop Pecham's 1279 monition to the nuns of Headingham that if they knew what was good for them, they would give in to the queen's wishes and admit a woman whose vocation Eleanor had decided to sponsor.[58] There can be little room for question that Queen Eleanor had a vengeful side, that she deployed her officials to coerce or punish on what amounted to a private basis and that her contemporaries, well aware of all of this, preferred to avoid her displeasure and advised others to do the same.

The administrative evidence we have been considering can reveal only its side of the woman, and it is a largely negative view. In the wardrobe records we encounter a different Eleanor of Castile: bountiful if cautious patroness of her kinfolk, energetic and discerning sponsor of

37

vernacular letters, the most active royal religious foundress in England since the reign of Henry I, an attentive mother and a wife rarely absent from her husband's side. To repeat details from these accounts would only increase our store of medieval trivia, so for the sake of brevity I will select a single incident at random and then suggest some of its ramifications. In 1286, King Edward gave his wife a set of chessmen in jasper and crystal. This reminds us that Eleanor's brother King Alphonso X wrote an important chess manual, and though we cannot prove she owned that work, Eleanor did once borrow from Cerne Abbey a volume that was probably the Anglo-Norman treatise on chess written at Cerne in her day.[59] That Eleanor sought written authority for the game's intricacies recalls the Anglo-Norman translation of Vegetius' Latin treatise *De Re Militari*, the medieval bible of chivalry, which she had one of her clerks prepare for Edward while they were on Crusade.[60] The same relationship in Eleanor's career between literature and the events of her life appears from the evidence for a lost 'romance about Isembart' she commissioned in Ponthieu shortly after she succeeded her mother in 1279: Isembart was a purely literary character invented by the creator of an early *chanson de geste*, but French chroniclers slowly transformed him into a count of Ponthieu, and the queen presumably saw him as one of her maternal ancestors.[61] The pattern behind such bits and pieces is that Eleanor was sufficiently accustomed to the use of writing to make it part of many areas of her life; the ample evidence for Eleanor's literary interests, including her personal scriptorium, is quite unambiguous and strongly suggests that she was following the example of her learned brother.[62]

The extent to which Eleanor's literate mentality informed her habits is also apparent in her spiritual life. In the 1280s the queen requested from Archbishop Pecham an explanation of some points in a complex theological work, the *Heavenly Hierarchy* of pseudo-Dionysius. The Primate answered with a short treatise on angels, which adds nothing to his literary reputation though it does indicate that the queen sought an informed understanding of the Church's teachings. This was in keeping with her devotion to the Preaching Friars, the Dominicans or Blackfriars, whose special ardor for scholastic endeavors made such significant contributions to learning in the thirteenth century. It is absurd to suggest that Eleanor participated personally in those intellectual developments, but she did apply her energies wholeheartedly to the Order's enrichment in England, founding three priories, increasing the lands of others and leaving rich legacies to all Dominican houses in England.[63] The king and queen had Dominican confessors and assigned friars to the household of their son; as the Preachers were known for their ideas on the teaching of children, these brothers were presumably intended to supervise the boy's education, in which one of Eleanor's scribes may have assisted.[64] The queen's private spiritual observances included saying the rosary, a relatively new form of devotion encouraged by the Dominicans, and she owned at least two books of hours from which she would have read the monastic office privately, another addition to the spiritual arsenal that was gaining popularity under the friars' influence. Eleanor's literate habits thus allowed her to benefit from the friars' new paths to spiritual development, an impulse she shared with many women for whom such private devotions offered a measure of freedom from male direction by a Church acutely distrustful of women.[65]

A queen's relationship with her offspring, especially her sons, was an important resource for her later years; supervising their education was one way to strengthen her influence in their lives, and the role of Eleanor's favored religious community in her son's training is one of many indications of her thoughtful attentiveness to her children's welfare. While Eleanor's maternal feelings have been questioned (on slim evidence),[66] her concern for her brood cannot be doubted. She objected strenuously in 1282 to the marriage of her thirteen-year-old daughter Eleanor because the girl was too young, an incident paralleled by her protests against another daughter's religious enclosure at the age of six.[67] The wardrobe accounts prove that messengers travelled regularly between the itinerant households of the king and queen and the children's less transient establishment, carrying the queen's enquiries about the children's health; their guardians were held strictly to account if they failed to inform the parents of their charges' progress.[68] One element can be said to have had a deleterious effect on the queen's relationship with her children: her endless travels did cause extended separations until the children were old enough to accompany the king and queen. While this must have affected all the children, it is naturally Edward of Caernarvon who attracts our attention. While his parents were in Aquitaine from 1286 until 1289, the child was separated from them between the ages of two and five and a half; by the time she returned to England in August 1289, Eleanor was fatally ill, and her death in November 1290 left the boy to face an ageing father he barely knew, with whom he never had a solid relationship.[69]

It can never be known whether Queen Eleanor's death removed what might have been a mediating presence between father and son. We can, however, place complete trust in the chroniclers' statements that Edward mourned Eleanor all his days. The two were parted in her lifetime only by childbirth, warfare, or diplomacy, and all evidence indicates that

39

their personal union was one of mutual affection and respect. A recurrent incident in the wardrobe accounts provides a rare personal glimpse into a medieval royal marriage: each year on the morning of Easter Monday, Eleanor's ladies-in-waiting stole into Edward's bedchamber and held him captive until he ransomed himself by paying them each £2. The explanation is that, like many medieval couples, Edward and Eleanor abstained from marital relations during Lent, so the queen's ladies doubtless found it a great joke to prevent the king from joining his wife after six weeks' continence.[70] The circumstances may strike modern ears as a bit racy, but the fact that the ladies were allowed to participate freely in the most intimate area of the royal marriage is a reminder that the medieval period regarded these matters with frankness, and we can suppose that such good-humored ease and freedom indicate a comfortable, secure relationship between king and queen. There is no reason to question the sincerity of Edward's much-quoted request of the abbot of Cluny six weeks after Eleanor's death, seeking prayers for the wife 'whom living we dearly cherished, and whom dead we cannot cease to love'.[71]

I draw to a close perched on the horns of a dilemma. Was Eleanor of Castile a vengeful and demanding queen as administrative evidence indicates, or was she rather the intelligent, amiable and gracious lady of the wardrobe records? If we are to resolve the dichotomy, all the evidence must be used with caution. What I mean can be shown by setting the evidence of the 1291 inquest in a wider, socially-constructed frame of reference. Eleanor appears as a grasping figure in complaints brought by those who lost lands to her, or from whom services or rents were detained or compelled - in other words, the landed class. In these complaints Eleanor is an immediate presence, spiteful in the Stockport case and even treacherous in that of John de Wauton, who (rather foolishly) asked for her help in clearing his debts to the Jewry. He received her assurance that he would not lose his lands in the process, but somehow his manor at West Betchworth quickly ended up in her hands.[72] In contrast, the complaints of poor tenants or townspeople involve the queen less than they do her officials; if Eleanor is mentioned in these complaints it is only as a remote and gracious figure to whom the poor appealed over the heads of abusive officials. Examples are the rector of Hanmer, who came to the queen at Macclesfield when the bailiffs at Overton detained him from his rights to fish in the queen's waters, or the townsmen of Overton who met with Eleanor at Clipston shortly before her death, seeking remedy for the bailiffs' excessive demands.[73] If we recall here that the chronicles critical of Queen Eleanor address her land hunger, and that the letters betraying fear of her wrath are from nobles and bishops, we can put this evidence in

40

a more secure context. The poor, socially and economically remote from the queen, had everything to hope for from her benevolence: projecting on her their expectations of mercy, they saw her as a benign and generous figure. In contrast, the knightly class shared with the queen a community of interests both cultural and economic, and had reason to be apprehensive about the way she used her office: they had the most to lose if she foreclosed on their estates or turned the king against them, choking off the flow of patronage from the Crown.[74]

That different views of Queen Eleanor are preserved by different kinds of documents, and that different social classes in the kingdom had contrasting opinions of her, are factors reflected in the evolution of her reputation over the centuries since her death. The wardrobe accounts' survival was a matter of such hazard that we are fortunate to have the few we now possess, and their contents were never widely known until the modern age rediscovered them. Nobody bothered to record what the lower classes thought of their king and queen, so the image of Queen Eleanor formed by tenants and townspeople was buried, encoded so to speak, in legal and administrative records that also lacked an audience. What did survive, for several decades at any rate, was the aristocratic memory of that greedy and vindictive Spaniard who despoiled honest Englishmen of their lands. But as the descendants of Eleanor's victims gradually abandoned their lawsuits, her methods were forgotten and by around 1400, her reputation was preserved solely by the crosses Edward raised along the route of her funeral procession and by the elaborate anniversary service he endowed at Westminster Abbey. That yearly commemoration is held to have influenced the proliferation of chantries in late medieval England, and it is true that in the years after Eleanor's death many people shrewdly obtained the king's licence to endow chantries by offering to include Eleanor among those for whose souls the chantry priests would celebrate. Located in churches around the kingdom, these chantries kept Eleanor's name alive in an impressive ritual context and may well have created an impression that her virtues were sufficient to inspire such widespread remembrance.[75]

Thus preserved by monument and religious commemoration, Eleanor's image was assuming a new guise when Thomas Walsingham wrote in the 1390s and this perhaps accounts for Walsingham's decision to copy a eulogy on Eleanor that originated in a St Albans work, today known as the *Opus chronicorum*, written in 1307-08. In sharp contrast to the silence about Eleanor that prevails in the chronicles written during her lifetime, the *Opus* acclaims her fulsomely at every opportunity: she

41

surpassed all women of her time in beauty, prudence and wisdom (indeed, she might be compared to the Sibyls), she was as a pillar of the realm, kept foreigners out of England and - of all things - protected the English from royal officials.[76] Now the fact that this chronicle was created within twenty years of Eleanor's death would seem to lend it considerable authority; but it is immediately obvious that its testimony accords ill with strictly contemporary evidence for current opinion about the queen. These anomalies can be explained by recalling that in 1308 there was a new king, Edward II, who most probably had only indistinct memories of his mother; the monks at St Albans were very likely out to flatter him by praising his mother in a work that was planned as a history of his father's reign and, plausibly, was intended to be presented to him. Walsingham may deserve full marks as a researcher for finding the *Opus* eulogy, but he must forfeit his claim as a reliable witness to popular opinion about Edward I's wife.

Between the mid-fourteenth and the late sixteenth century, references to Eleanor of Castile become increasingly rare in chronicles and documents. She is properly mentioned as Edward's wife and the mother of his successor, but chroniclers cease to concern themselves with the details of her life and by the late fifteenth century she is no more than a name in the many genealogical rolls of the royal lineage produced in that period.[77] By that time, too, the Eleanor crosses may have lost some of their hold on popular imagination. At least two of them were sadly dilapidated by the mid-fifteenth century; William Worcestre's *Itineraries* mention none of them, while Leland's *Itinerary* refers to only one without identifying the queen whom it commemorated.[78] Then, in 1574, Walsingham's chronicle was printed; Ralph Holinshed's compilation of English chronicles, published in 1577, gave an English version of Walsingham's Latin and helped circulate the pirated St Albans eulogy more widely.[79] The dissemination of the eulogy may have been the spark that rekindled interest in the long-dead queen; the text clearly attracted the attention of the prince of English antiquarians, William Camden, who has the distinction of discovering, in a fourteenth-century Italian chronicle, the legend that Eleanor rescued Edward at Acre by sucking his wounds.[80] Camden was neither the first nor the last to weave whole cloth out of few threads, but in every essential it was he who, with *Britannia* (1586), created the long-current image of Eleanor of Castile by bringing together for the first time Walsingham's indisputably medieval eulogy, the Acre fable and the monumental testimony of the Eleanor crosses - the three elements upon which the queen's reputation has rested for so long.[81]

The popularisation of Camden's account of Eleanor is best seen in James Thomson's 1739 dramatisation of the Acre legend. Eleanor is told by Daraxa, a captive Arab princess, that Edward can be saved if someone sucks the poison from his wounds, but whoever does so will surely die. Hesitating only long enough to deliver an impassioned monologue, Eleanor saves her husband's life; as she lies dying the Sultan Selim, impressed by her heroic devotion, enters the crusaders' camp disguised as a dervish and administers an antidote to the fatal venom. Edward's tribute to his faithful wife moves us, not necessarily in the direction the playwright intended: 'This Partner of my Soul! Such a mild Light / Of careless Charms, of unaffected Beauty, / Such more than Beauty, such endearing Goodness, / That when I meet her Eye, where cordial Faith, / And every gentle Virtue mix their Lustre, / I feel a Transport that partakes of Anguish!'[82] By the mid-eighteenth century, too, interest in the Eleanor crosses was growing; engravings of them were published from 1718, followed by the Society of Antiquaries' *Vetusta Monumenta* (1780). The first efforts to repair the crosses (1713) inaugurated a series of restoration projects that have continued to the present day, and by 1796 the monuments were seemingly well enough known to the public to furnish subject matter for Cruikshank's satirical engraving showing a group of antiquarians poring over the cross at Waltham.[83] The nineteenth century's cult of the medieval nourished an even more passionate interest in the crosses, which were the model for the Martyrs' Memorial at Oxford and influenced the design of the Albert Memorial in London by Gilbert Scott, who called the crosses 'the most touching monuments ever erected in this country to a Royal Consort'.[84]

With such passages as Thompson's in circulation and such public interest in the crosses we cannot be very surprised that so dedicated a literata and so devoted a romantic as Agnes Strickland dipped her pen in syrup to describe Queen Eleanor, though other factors did play a part in determining the tone of Strickland's work. Her staunch Anglican and Tory sympathies, for example, did much to shape (not to say deform) her view of the medieval period. Strickland claimed noble descent and wrote as one to the manner born who aimed her work at a congenially gentle audience; the *Lives* mirror values she took to be shared by the gentry, though the work's domestic focus and fulsome moralising point to a rather closer connection with the Victorian middle class.[85] To give her credit Strickland did admit that the Acre story was improbable, but for the rest her account of Eleanor of Castile is so thoroughly saturated with the spirit of William Camden that it ignores contradictory evidence accessible in Strickland's time: the Hundred Rolls, Parliament Rolls, and the Guisborough chronicle were all available either for her first edition or for the later revisions, but Strickland never mentions them. Far more serious, in the case of one who repeatedly asserted that her work was based on original evidence, was Strickland's selective use of the published sources she did consult. From the accounts of Eleanor's executors, for example, Strickland was happy to cite evidence that the queen owned books and other objects of refinement; but those accounts also record payments for damages awarded during the inquest of 1291, and the reason for those payments is explicitly stated in the accounts. Miss Strickland ignores those entries, and fails to note that the inquest ever took place.[86]

All of which serves to explain how and why we have inherited a misleading and one-dimensional picture of Eleanor of Castile, but it still does not answer the main question: what kind of woman was she? The evidence as a whole reveals an intelligent, well-educated woman of sufficient vigor and firmness to meet the demands of the position the diplomatic lottery thrust upon her - not in themselves bad qualities, though they can be manifest in unpleasant ways. As I have sought to show, a medieval queen occupied a position of great honor and wealth, but it was also an office of considerable uncertainty. Much depended on the skill and application with which a queen created and sustained impressions of power; to borrow a modern phrase, it was very much a case of use it or lose it. And however guarded a view we may take of certain of her actions, it has to be acknowledged that Eleanor of Castile's response to the exigencies of her position was decided and effective. An early twentieth-century popular biographer of English kings might lament that 'cold research' was beginning to tarnish Eleanor's image as 'the loving and selfless being of our dreams',[87] but if a purely subjective opinion may be ventured after nearly twenty years' acquaintance, the spirited Eleanor of the record evidence emerges as a far more absorbing woman than the cloying consort described by Strickland or Thomas Costain.

Certainly no one will deny that Eleanor succeeded in the most crucial of her obligations, as a wife and mother, and it is well to conclude by giving the last word to the husband on whose life Eleanor had the greatest impact. Mention has already been made of the yearly Easter attack on Edward by the queen's ladies, and what it tells us about their marriage. At Easter 1291 the queen was five months dead, her ladies re-assigned to her daughters' chambers, and there was no reason for them to trap the king; but on that Easter Monday, Edward gave the seven ladies his ransom as was the custom when the queen was alive.[88] In Eleanor's lifetime, the ladies' invasion was a pleasant ritual of annual renewal; now it showed how difficult Edward was finding it to detach himself from her and all she had meant in his life. It is common nowadays to describe the Eleanor crosses as part of a program of dynastic glorification Edward undertook in the 1290s, and there is good evidence for that theory; but such ideas do seem to lose a little of their force in the face of this gesture that shows so clearly the human feelings involved. Surely, we cannot withhold our respect from the woman whose life merited such a last remembrance.

Notes

Abbreviations

CChR	*Calendar of Charter Rolls*
CClR	*Calendar of Close Rolls*
CFR	*Calendar of Fine Rolls*
CPR	*Calendar of Patent Rolls*
MGH, SS	*Monumenta Germaniae Historica, Scriptores*
RP, Rot. Parl.	*Rotuli Parliamentorum*
VCH	*Victoria County History*

[1] H. Johnstone, 'Archbishop Pecham and the Council of Lambeth of 1281', in *Essays in Mediaeval History presented to Thomas Frederick Tout*, ed. A. G. Little, F. M. Powicke (Manchester, 1925), pp.171-88; V. Galbraith, 'Good Kings and Bad Kings in Medieval English History', *History*, 30 (1945), pp.119-32.

[2] A. Strickland, *Lives of the Queens of England*, 12 vols. (London, 1840-48), cited here in 2nd edn., 8 vols. (London, 1851, reissued 1854). A useful account of Strickland's life, work and methods is U. Pope-Hennessy, *Agnes Strickland: Biographer of the Queens of England (1796-1874)* (London, 1940).

[3] J. C. Parsons, *The Court and Household of Eleanor of Castile in 1290* (Toronto, 1977), pp.6-27; 'The Year of Eleanor of Castile's Birth, and her Children by Edward I', *Mediaeval Studies*, 46 (1984), pp.245-65; 'The Beginnings of English Administration in Ponthieu: an Unnoticed Document of 1280', *Mediaeval Studies*, 50 (1988), pp.371-403; M. Prestwich, *Edward I* (Berkeley, CA, 1988), passim, esp. pp.123-26; B. and C. R. Byerly, *Records of the Wardrobe and Household, 1285-1286* (London, 1977), and *Records of the Wardrobe and Household, 1286-1289* (London, 1986).

[4] *Annales Prioratus de Dunstaplia*, ed. H. Luard (Rolls series, 36.2. London, 1866), p.362; *The Chronicle of Walter of Guisborough*, ed. H. Rothwell (Camden, 3rd series, 89, 1957), p. 216 (author's translation); *Registrum Epistolarum Fratris Johannis Peckham Archiepiscopi Cantuariensis*, ed. C. T. Martin, 3 vols. (Rolls series, 77. London, 1882-84), 2, pp.555, 619-20, 937.

[5] Sharon Farmer, 'Persuasive Voices: Clerical Images of Medieval Wives', *Speculum*, 61 (1986), pp.517-43.

[6] J. Wickham Legg, ed., *English Coronation Records* (Westminster, 1901), pp.37, 100; *Roberti Grosseteste Epistolae*, ed. H. Luard (Rolls series, 25. London, 1861), pp.271-72, 310-11); *Reg. Peckham*, 2, p.555.

[7] *Gesta Abbatum Sancti Albani*, ed. H. T. Riley, 3 vols. (Rolls series, 28. London, 1867-69), pp.411-12. I have dealt in a series of papers with intercessory activity by the thirteenth-century English queens; my article on the subject is forthcoming among papers from a February 1990 conference at the University of Toronto.

[8] R. F. Treharne, *The Baronial Plan of Reform, 1258-1263* (Manchester, 1932), p.308, feels that while the extent of Eleanor of Provence's influence is unclear, contemporaries' impressions of her meddling cannot be questioned.

[9] References to ceremonial receptions of the king and queen are, e.g., *Chron. of Bury*, ed. A. Gransden (London, 1964) pp.57, 66, 83, 92; *Ann. Monasterii de Wintonia*, ed. H. Luard (Rolls Series, 36.2 London, 1865) p.120; *Ann. de Dunstaplia*, pp.266, 355; *Ann. Prioratus de Oseneia*, ed. Luard (Rolls series, 36.4. London, 1869), pp.268, 278-79, 325; *Ann. Monasterii de Waverleia*, ed. Luard (Rolls Series 36.2. London, 1865) pp.391, 402; *The Chronicle of Glastonbury Abbey: an edition, translation and study of John of Glastonbury's Cronica sive Antiquitates Glastoniensis Ecclesie*, ed. J. P. Carley, trs. D. Townsend (Woodbridge, 1985), pp.243, 245. Some idea of the elaborate ritual on such occasions can be seen in the fourteenth-century *Liber Pontificalis of Edmund Lacy, Bishop of Exeter*, ed. R. Barnes (Exeter, 1847), p.280.

[10] P. Stafford, *Queens, Concubines and Dowagers: the King's Wife in the Early Middle Ages* (Athens, GA, 1985); M. Facinger, 'A Study in Queenship: Capetian France', *Studies in Medieval and Renaissance History*, 5 (1968), pp.1-47; J. C. Parsons, 'Eleanor of Castile (1241-1290) and the English Queenship in the Thirteenth Century', Ph.D. diss., University of Toronto (1980).

[11] For Berengaria, J. Gillingham, 'Richard I and Berengaria of Navarre', *Bull. Inst. of Historical Research*, 53 (1980), pp.157-73; for Isabella, K. Norgate, *The Minority of Henry III* (London, 1912), pp.55, 134; S. Painter, *The Reign of King John* (Baltimore, 1949), pp.227, 235-36; W. L. Warren, *King John* (London, 1961), pp.75, 139.

[12] Eleanor of Aquitaine was remarkably active and influential after Henry II's death, but her political behavior as dowager cannot be considered in the same light as that of a queen-consort whose husband was living. Her position after 1189 resulted from a unique combination of circumstances, as properly emphasized by H. G. Richardson and G. O. Sayles, *The Governance of England from the Conquest to Magna Carta* (Edinburgh, 1963), p.153.

[13] *Documents of the Baronial Movement of Reform and Rebellion, 1258-1267*, ed. R. F. Treharne, I. J. Sanders (Oxford, 1973), pp.78-79; cf. M. Howell, 'The Resources of Eleanor of Provence as Queen Consort', *Eng. Hist. Review*, 102 (1987), pp.372-93.

[14] Th. Rymer, *Foedera, Conventiones, Litterae*, 4 vols. in 7 (Record Commn. London, 1816-69), 1, p.495.

¹⁵ *Henry of Pytchley's Book of Fees*, ed. W. T. Mellows (Northampton Record Society, **2**, 1927), pp.64, 71-72; *CPR 1281-1292*, p.414.

¹⁶ E.g., Byerly, *Records, 1285-1286*, nos. 1983, 1988, 1989, 1991, 2006.

¹⁷ J. C. Parsons, 'Eleanor of Castile and the Viscountess Jeanne of Châtelleraut', *Genealogists' Magazine*, **23** (1989), pp.141-44; *CPR 1258-1266*, pp.212-13, 376-77; *Records of the Trial of Walter Langeton, Bishop of Coventry and Lichfield 1307-1312*, ed. A. Beardwood (Camden Society, 4th series, **6**, 1969), pp.106-7 (cf. *Cal. Inqs. Post Mortem*, **4**, no. 456); B. Botfield and Th. Turner, *Manners and Household Expenses of England in the Thirteenth and Fifteenth Centuries* (Roxburghe Club, London, 1841), p.104 (cf. *Cal. Inqs. Post Mortem*, **2**, no. 266); S. L. Waugh, *The Lordship of England: Royal Wardships and Marriages in English Society and Politics, 1217-1327* (Princeton, 1988), esp. pp.191-92, 214-15.

¹⁸ Paris, *Chron. Majora*, **5**, pp.513-14; M. Ridgeway, 'Foreign Favourites and Henry III's Problems of Patronage, 1247-1258', *Eng. Hist. Rev.*, **104** (1989), pp.590-616; J. C. Holt, 'Feudal Society and the Family in Early Medieval England: iv. The Heiress and the Alien', *Trans. Royal Hist. Society*, 5th ser., **35** (1985), pp.1-28; S. L. Waugh, 'Marriage, Class and Royal Lordship in England under Henry III', *Viator*, **16** (1985), pp.181-208.

¹⁹ J. C. Parsons, *The Court and Household of Eleanor of Castile in 1290* (Toronto, 1977), pp.41-55; 'Eleanor of Castile and the Countess Margaret of Ulster', *Genealogists' Magazine*, **20** (June 1982), pp.335-40.

²⁰ *CClR 1264-1268*, p.28, implies that Edward granted her the manor, but a later enrolment (E 159/60, m. 4) states that Henry made the grant at Edward's instance.

²¹ P.R.O., S.C. 1/11/25, dated from *CPR 1258-1266*, pp.453, 476; edited in *Royal and other Historical Letters illustrative of the Reign of Henry III*, ed. W. W. Shirley, 2 vols. (Rolls series, **27**. London, 1862-66), no. 647, English translation at **2**, pp.370-71.

²² In Henry III's reign £1000 yearly was the amount deemed adequate for the queen's needs when out of court, but even then that sum was insufficient; Howell, 'The Resources of Eleanor of Provence as Queen Consort', pp.372-93, esp. pp.387-88; Parsons, *Eleanor of Castile and the English Queenship*, esp. ch. 2; *Court and Household*, esp. p.154 note.

²³ Parsons, *Court and Household*, pp.154-60; *Eleanor of Castile and the English Queenship*, p.187.

²⁴ For the dower assignment, *CChR*, **2**, pp.192-93; Parsons, *Eleanor of Castile and the English Queenship*, p.199. The £8000 included £4937 8s. 6d. out of the queen's treasury, and wardrobe expenses of £1009 12s.11¼d. (*Court and Household*, p.134). In 1289-90 her servants' clothing cost the king £1569 (*Eleanor of Castile and the English Queenship*, p.187).

²⁵ Parsons, *Eleanor of Castile and the English Queenship*, pp.198-99.

[26] For Eleanor of Provence's dower assignment made in 1262 to supersede that made on her marriage in 1236, *CPR 1258-1266*, pp.736-37 (where the initial reference to '£10,000' is plainly an error for '£1000').

[27] *CClR 1279-1288*, pp.80-81.

[28] Eleanor's mother's physician was a Jew (G. Sánchez de la Cuesta y Gutierrez, *Dos Reyes Enfermos del Corazón: los Conquistadores de Sevilla* [Seville, 1948], p.46; L. Fernandez de Retana, *Albores del Império. San Fernando III y su epoca* [Madrid, 1941], p.405). For the Jews' role in Castilian royal financial administration, E. Mayer, *História de las instituciones sociales y políticos de España, siglos v-xiv*, 2 vols. (Madrid, 1935), 2, p. 54.

[29] After 1272, Eleanor twice tried to appoint Jews as her goldkeepers: Jacob de Oxonia on 1 March 1273 (Walter de Guldeford' was substituted 5 August 1273; E 159/57, mm. 7, 5); and in Trinity term 1276, Benedict de Winton', 'as other Jews have always been accustomed to do' (E 159/59, m. 8d, likewise ineffective). But no other Jew is known to have filled that office unless Eleanor used them for her Irish gold between 1268 and 1272 (*CPR 1266-1272*, p.198; *Cal. Docts. relating to Ireland*, 1, no. 889 [p.146]).

[30] I owe to Margaret Howell the valuable suggestion that there may have been a relationship between the attitudes shown to the Jewry by the two Eleanors, and their respective sympathies to the Franciscan and Dominican orders (for Eleanor of Castile's Dominican patronage, above, pp.38-39). See, in general, Jeremy Cohen, *The Friars and the Jews. The Evolution of Medieval Anti-Judaism* (Ithaca, N.Y., 1982); Yitzhak Baer, *A History of the Jews in Christian Spain*, trs. L. Shoffman, 2 vols. (Philadelphia, 1961-66), 1, pp.111-37.

[31] *CPR 1272-1281*, p.433 (= *Foedera*, 1, p.591).

[32] C. Roth, *The Jews of Medieval Oxford* (Oxford, 1951); H. P. Stokes, 'The Relationship between the Jews and the Royal Family of England in the Thirteenth Century', *Transactions of the Jewish Historical Society of England*, 8 (1915-1917), pp.171-88.

[33] C. Picciotto, 'The Legal Position of the Jews in Pre-expulsion England', *Trans. Jewish Historical Society of England*, 9 (1918-20), pp.67-85; H. G. Richardson, *The English Jewry under the Angevin Kings* (London, 1960), pp.100-2, 107, 270-71, 275-80; *Select Pleas, Starrs and other Records*, ed. Rigg, introduction, appendix iii.

[34] The 1281 list of Eleanor's new manors has examples of Jewish debts reaching her hands both through queen-gold and the king's grants (*CPR 1279-1288*, pp.80-81).

[35] *CClR 1279-1288*, pp.80-81 gives several examples.

[36] L. Ehrlich, *Proceedings against the Crown, 1216-1377* (Oxford, 1921), pp.206-11; *Select Cases in the Court of King's Bench in the Reign of Edward I*, ed. G. O. Sayles, 3 (Selden Society, 58, 1939), p.xlvi note 10.

[37] *CPR 1279-1288*, p.80; S. Raban, 'The Land Market and the Aristocracy in the Thirteenth Century', in *Tradition and Change: Essays in Honour of Marjorie Chibnall*,

ed. D. Greenaway, C. Holdsworth, J. Sayers (Cambridge, 1985), pp.239-61, esp. p.242.

[38] F. M. Powicke, *King Henry III and the Lord Edward*, 2 vols. (Oxford, 1947), p.704.

[39] *CPR 1272-1281*, p.265; *CFR 1272-1307*, p.97. This grant included both Cawston and John de Burgh's manor of Camel in Somerset, also surrendered in 1273 and hence part of the queen's dower assignment. Eleanor held Camel at pleasure from April 1276 (*CPR 1272-1281*, p.139; *CFR 1272-1307*, p.68). For Scottow, *CClR 1272-1279*, p.205, and *CClR 1279-1288*, p.80.

[40] For lands at Burgh, *CClR 1279-1279*, p.497; for the Scottow ejections, *CPR 1281-1292*, p.207; *CClR 1296-1302*, pp.415-16; *CClR 1302-1307*, pp.39-40.

[41] *CClR 1279-1288*, p.81; *Pedes Finium for the County of Somerset, 1196-1307*, ed. E. Green (Somerset Record Society, 1892), p.318; *Cal. of Memoranda Rolls (Exchequer), Michaelmas 1326-1327* (London [H.M.S.O.], 1968), no. 815; *Placitorum Abbreviatio, Richard I-Edward II* (London [Record Commn.], 1811), p.256; *Memoranda de Parliamento. Records of the Parliament holden at Westminster 28 February, 33 Edward I*, ed. F. W. Maitland (Rolls series, 98. London, 1893), p.158.

[42] For Leyburn, *CClR 1272-1279*, pp.221, 499; *CClR 1279-1288*, p.80; *Cal. of Pleas in the Exchequer of the Jews*, ed. J. M. Rigg, H. Jenkinson *et al.*, 4 vols. to date (Jewish Historical Society of England. London, 1920f), 3, pp. 78-79; *CPR 1272-1279*, p.335. For Crevequer, *Cal. Pleas in the Exchequer of the Jews*, 3, pp.110-11; *CPR 1272-1281*, p.283; *CPR 1272-1281*, pp.334-35.

[43] *CCR 1272-1279*, p.498; *CClR 1279-1288*, p.80; *CChR*, 2, p.357; *Cal. Inqs. Post Mortem*, 1, no. 563.

[44] Prestwich, *Edward I*, pp.103-5.

[45] Westminster Abbey, Muniments 5144; I am grateful to Mr N. H. MacMichael F.S.A., Keeper of the Muniments, for drawing the document to my attention.

[46] *CClR 1272-1279*, pp.577-78; *CClR 1279-1288*, p.80. The queen paid for the candles at his funeral in 1286 (Byerly, *Records 1286-1289*, no. 3114).

[47] G. Wrottesley, *Pedigrees from the Plea Rolls* (London, n.d.), pp.553-54; *CClR 1296-1302*, pp.72-73, *V.C.H. Warkwicks.*, 3, p.98; *CClR 1337-1339*, p.256; *CClR 1337-1339*, p.510; *CPR 1340-1343*, p.367; *Rot. Parl.*, 2, p.48, and *VCH Herts.*, 2 p.292.

[48] Parsons, *Court and Household*, pp.20-21, 137-52.

[49] Respectively: *Cal. Inqs. Miscellaneous*, 1, nos. 1184, 875 (for the relief, E 13/6, m. 9); *Rot. Hund.*, 2, pp.4-5; *Calendar of County Court, City Court and Eyre Rolls of Chester, 1259-1297*, ed. R. Stewart-Brown (Chetham Society, N.S. 84, 1925), pp.212, 213, 225; *CClR 1272-1279*, p.70, and *CClR 1279-1288*, p.16; *Cal. Inqs. Post Mortem*, 2, no. 619; *Rot. Parl.* 1, pp.50 *bis*, pp.299, 310; *CPR 1281-1292*, pp.330-31; *Cal. Inqs. Post Mortem*, 5, no. 137, and *Rôles gascons*, 2, no. 1570; *CPR 1281-1292*, p.210.

[50] H. Johnstone, 'The Queen's Household', in T. F. Tout, *Chapters in the Administrative History of Medieval England*, 6 vols. (Manchester, 1929-1933), 5, pp.270-72; M. E. Fenwick, 'The Inquiry into Complaints against the Ministers of Eleanor of Castile, 1291-92', unpublished M.A. thesis (University of London, 1931); N. M. Fryde, 'A Royal Enquiry into Abuses: Queen Eleanor's Ministers in North-East Wales, 1291-92', *Welsh History Review*, 5 (1970-71), pp.366-76.

[51] Such complaints against Lovetot were proved at Cawston and Burgh (J.I. 1/836, mm. 2, 6d), and in the New Forest (J.I. 1/1014, mm. 1d, 7). A justice of the Common Pleas from 1275, Lovetot was disgraced in the judicial scandal of 1289-93 (*State Trials of the Reign of Edward I, 1289-93* , ed. T. F. Tout and H. Johnstone [Camden Society, 3rd ser., 9, 1906], pp.236-39).

[52] Kancia is noted below; for Bures, Fryde, 'A Royal Enquiry into Abuses', *passim*. On Ponte, *CClR 1279-1288*, p.88 (cf. *CPR 1266-1272*, p.459, *CChR*, 2, pp.190-91); on Kancia, *A Calendar of New Forest Documents*, 1: *1244-1334*, ed. D. J. Stagg (Hants. County Council, Record ser., 3, 1979), nos. 117, 179-85, 190, 212, 249; *CClR 1272-1279*, p.349; *RO*, 1, p.47; *CClR 1288-1296*, pp.82, 113; *RP*, 1, p.299; *CPR 1281-1292*, p.212. Ponte was Kancia's executor (J.I. 1/542, m. 5), so they may have been related and Ponte perhaps came from Bridge in Kent.

[53] For Lovetot, J.I. 1/542, mm. 4d, 12; Ponte, J.I. 1/542, m. 5d; Taverner, J.I. 1/1149, m. 1d. Stagg, *NFD*, 1, nos. 95, 212, 249; *CClR 1279-1288*, p. 2; for the testament of John de Badesleye, Stagg, nos. 192, 193, 249. The executor obtained restitution only in 1291 (J.I. 1/1014, m. 8d).

[54] Ehrlich, *Proceedings against the Crown*, pp.206-11.

[55] *CPR 1281-1292*, p.405. The officials of prominent nobles, including Henry III's brother Richard of Cornwall, were occasionally brought to book (*CClR 1259-1261*, p.335; *CPR 1258-1266*, p. 657).

[56] J.I. 1/1149, m. 2d (where the statement that the bailiff testified in secret is carefully interlined). Stokepord also presented Kancia to the rectory of Prestbury c.1275 (*The Chartulary or Register of the Abbey of St Werburgh, Chester*, ed. J. Tait, 2 vols. [Chetham Society, N.S. 79, 82, Manchester, 1920-23], 2, no. 574).

[57] *The Register of Bishop Godfrey Giffard of Worcester, 1268-1302*, ed. J. W. Willis Bund (Worcester Historical Society, 1898), pp.175-76.

[58] *Reg. Peckham* (RS 77), 1, pp.56-57.

[59] Byerly, *Records 1286-1289*, no. 2009. Eleanor's undated letter thanking the abbot of Cerne for sending her the book 'sicut petivimus' is on J.I. 1/1014, m. 1; on the Cerne treatise, R. Eales, 'The Game of Chess: An Aspect of Medieval Knightly Culture', in *The Ideals and Practice of Knighthood: Papers from the first and second Strawberry Hill Conferences*, ed. C. Harper-Bill and R. Harvey (Woodbridge, 1986), pp.12-34, esp. p.28.

[60] L. Thorpe, 'Mastre Richard, a Thirteenth Century Translator of the '"De Re Militari" of Vegetius', *Scriptorium*, 6 (1952), pp.39-50, and 'Mastre Richard at the Skirmish of Kenilworth?', *ibid.*, 7 (1953), pp.120-21; M. D. Legge, 'The Lord Edward's Vegetius', *ibid.*, 7 (1953), pp.262-65; J. Folda, *Crusader Manuscript*

Illumination at Saint-Jean d'Acre, 1275-1291 (Princeton, 1976), pp.16-17, 129-30, 199. On the appeal of Vegetius in the medieval period, M. Keen, *Chivalry* (New Haven, 1984), pp.111-12.

61 J. C. Parsons, 'The Beginnings of English Administration in Ponthieu', esp. pp.376, 395, 398.

62 Parsons, *Court and Household*, pp.13-14; Byerly, *Records 1285-1286*, no. 2368, and *Records 1286-1289*, nos. 208, 3207, 3210, 3213-14, 3217, 3220, 3223-24, 3226-27, 3234, 3236, 3238, 3239-40, 3246; Botfield, *Manners*, pp.103, 104, 139.

63 Parsons, *Court and Household*, pp.16-17; *CPR 1272-1281*, p.322; *CChR*, 2, p.345 (Salisbury); *Entries in the Papal Registers relating to Great Britain and Ireland*, ed. W. H. Bliss *et al.*, 15 vols. to date (London [H.M.S.O.], 1894f), 2, pp.207, 217, and 5, pp.501-2; Botfield, *Manners*, pp.96, 102-3.

64 For the confessors, Parsons, *Court and Household*, p.127 and note, and Byerly, *Records 1285-1286*, no. 400; friars in Edward of Caernarvon's household are noted in 1289-90 (C 47/4/5, fols. 13, 29). For Eleanor's scribe sent to young Edward's household at Woodstock in 1290, *Court and Household*, pp.95-96.

65 For rosaries, Byerly, *Records 1286-1289*, no. 3241, and Parsons, *Court and Household*, pp.80, 106; for books of hours, Botfield, *Manners*, p.136. See R. S. Wieck, *Time Sanctified: The Book of Hours in Medieval Art and Life* (New York-Baltimore, 1988), incl. L. R. Poos, 'Social History and the Book of Hours', esp. pp.34-35, and V. Reinburg, 'Prayer and the Book of Hours', esp. pp.39-40; S. G. Bell, 'Medieval Women Book Owners', in *Sisters and Workers in the Middle Ages*, ed. J. M. Bennett *et al.* (Chicago, 1989), pp.135-61, esp. pp.146-50.

66 Johnstone, 'Archbishop Pecham and the Council of Lambeth of 1281', p.171, 'marvelled' that Eleanor was absent from her son's deathbed in 1274, though Johnstone in 1923 had offered a less censorious explanation ('The Wardrobe and Household of Henry, son of Edward I', *Bull. John Rylands Library*, 7 [1923], pp.395-96). The boy Henry did not die alone at Guildford in October 1274; Guildford was a dower residence of his grandmother Eleanor of Provence (*CPR 1258-1266*, p.737), and S.C. 1/22/29, a letter from that queen dated at Guildford on a 14 October (no year), deals with business of Henry of Almain's widow Constance and was probably sent in 1274 (cf. *CPR 1272-1281*, pp.58, 63-64).

67 *Rôles gascons*, 2, no. 597 (this daughter was born in June 1269, not 1264 as is commonly stated: Parsons, 'The Year of Eleanor of Castile's Birth', p.260).

68 Johnstone, 'The Wardrobe and Household of Henry', p.397 note 4, p.400; Byerly, *Records 1285-1286*, no. 66, and *Records 1286-1289*, nos. 1060, 3229. Edward scolded the governess of his children by his second wife when the woman forgot to send him word of their welfare (P. Chaplais, 'Some Personal Letters of Edward I', *Eng. Hist. Rev.*, 77 [1962], pp.79-86, esp. 86).

69 H. Johnstone, *Edward of Carnarvon* (Manchester, 1944).

70 We hear of this in 1278 (C 47/4/1, fol. 27v), 1287 (Byerly, *Records 1286-1289*, no. 980), and 1290 (C 47/4/5, fol. 45v). See A. Vauchez, *Les laïcs au moyen age: Pratiques et expériences religieuses* (Paris, 1987), pp.203-9; D. Weinstein and R. M.

Bell, *Saints and Society: the Two Worlds of Western Christendom, 100-1700* (Chicago, 1986), pp.75-81.

[71] *Foedera*, **1**, p. 743.

[72] J.I. 1/542 m. 4d. Shortly after Wauton met with the queen, he contracted a fresh debt to Hagin f. Cresseus, so intimately linked with Eleanor's affairs that he was known as 'the queen's Jew' (*Select Pleas, Starrs and Other Records from the Rolls of the Exchequer of the Jews, A.D. 1220-1284*, ed. J. M. Rigg [Selden Society **15**, 1902] pp.87-88; *CPR 1281-1292*, p.384). Within a few weeks Hagin conveyed that debt to the queen, who thus obtained Betchworth (E 9/47, mm. 3d, 5d, 9, 9d). There is more than a hint here of collusion between Eleanor and Hagin. I am grateful to Mr Paul Brand for allowing me to consult his transcripts of unpublished rolls of the Exchequer of the Jews.

[73] J.I. 1/1149, mm. 6, 10. Independent record evidence shows that she once agreed to reduce the rent demanded from poor tenants in Anglesey (*List of Welsh Entries in the Memoranda Rolls, 1282-1343*, ed. N. Fryde, [Cardiff, 1974], no. 144).

[74] J. C. Parsons, 'Earthly Queen, Heavenly Queen: appeal and intercession in medieval England', unpublished paper read at the Twenty-fourth International Congress on Medieval Studies, Western Michigan University, Kalamazoo, Michigan (May 1989).

[75] G. H. Cook, *Mediaeval Chantries and Chantry Chapels*, 2nd ed. (London, 1963), p.8 (cf. *CChR*, **2**, pp.411, 424-26); cf. F. D. Blackley, 'Isabella of France, Queen of England (1308-1358) and the late medieval cult of the dead', *Canadian Journal of History*, **15** (1980), pp.23-47. For foundations in memory of Queen Eleanor, *CPR 1281-1292*, p.414, *Henry of Pytchley's Book of Fees*, ed. Mellows, pp.71-72, and *Antient Kalendars and Inventories of the Treasury of His Majesty's Exchequer*, ed. F. Palgrave, 3 vols. (Record Commn. London, 1836), **1**, p.110; *CPR 1292-1301*, p.54, and *Rolls and Register of Bishop Oliver Sutton*, ed. Hill, **2**, p.120; *Descriptive Catalogue of Ancient Deeds*, 6 vols. (H.M.S.O., 1890-1915), **3**, p.316; *CPR 1301-1307*, pp.316-17; *CPR 1281-1292*, p.487; *CPR 1292-1301*, p.26; *CPR 1321-1324*, p.324.

[76] The St Albans eulogy passed through three stages: (i) anon., 1307-08, *Opus chronicorum*, ed. H. T. Riley in *Johannis de Trokelowe et Henrici de Blaneford. . . necnon quorundam anonymorum chronica et annales* (Rolls series, **28**.3. London, 1866), pp.26, 47-48, 49-50; (ii) anon., after 1327, *Willelmi Rishanger Chronica*, ed. Riley in *Willelmi Rishanger. . . et quorundam anonymorum chronica et annales regnantibus Henrico III et Edwardo I* (Rolls series, **28**.2. London, 1865), pp.210-21; (iii) after 1392, *Thome Walsingham quondam monachi sancti Albani Historia Anglicana*, ed. Riley, 2 vols. (Rolls series, **28**.1. London, 1863-64), **1**, p.32, repeating verbatim the text in (ii).

[77] On the proliferation of royal genealogies in the fifteenth century, R. A. Griffiths, 'The Sense of Dynasty in the Reign of Henry VI', pp.13-16, and A. Allen, 'Yorkist Propaganda: Pedigree, Prophecy and the 'British History' in the Reign of Edward IV', pp.171-92, both in C. Ross, ed., *Patronage, Pedigree and Power in Later Medieval England* (Gloucester, 1979).

[78] William Worcestre, *Itineraries* (ed. J. H. Harvey. Oxford, 1969); *The Itinerary of John Leland in or about the years 1535-1543*, ed. L. T. Smith, 5 vols. (London, 1907-10), **1**, p.8 (cf. **1**, pp.310-11, and **5**, p.201). The Hardingstone cross was 'headless' in 1460 (R. M. Serjeantson, *History of Delapré Abbey* [Northampton, 1909], p.23), and in 1441 the Chepe cross in London was 'by length of time decayed'. Its periodic refurbishings were expressions of London's civic pride unrelated to Queen Eleanor's reputation (*Stow's Survey of London* [1598], ed. H. B. Wheatley [London, 1956], pp.238-39).

[79] R. Holinshed, *Chronicles of England, Scotland and Ireland* (originally London, 1577; repr. in 6 vols., London, 1807-1808), **2**, pp.431, 435, 439.

[80] The story first occurs in the *Historia Ecclesiastica* written in the 1320s by the Italian Dominican, Bartolomeo Fiadoni (Ptolemy) of Lucca, but its genesis is shrouded in mystery and we shall doubtless never know how Fiadoni came by it (*Rerum Italicarum Scriptores*, ed. L. A. Muratori, 25 vols. in 28 [Milan, 1723-51], **11**, col.1168, where the story is reported only as popular tradition ['Tradunt autem. . . .']). Fiadoni omitted the legend from his *Brevis Annales*, ed. B. Schmiedler, *MGH, SS* new ser., **8** (1955), pp.169-71.

[81] William Camden, *Britannia* (London, 1586; rpt., ed. E. Gibson, 2 vols., London, 1722), **1**, cols. 390-91, and *Remains of a Larger Work Concerning Britain*, ed. R. D. Dunn (Toronto, 1984), pp.236-37, 444.

[82] J. Thomson, *Edward and Eleanora, a Tragedy, by Mr Thomson* (London, 1739); the passage quoted is from Act 2, scene iii (pp. 21-22).

[83] Society of Antiquaries of London, *Vetusta Monumenta quae ad rerum Britannicarum memoriam conservandam Societas antiquariorum Londini sumptu suo edenda curavit*, 7 vols. (London, 1747-1835), esp. vol. 2 (1780). Cruikshank's caricature is noted by A. Pope, 'Queen Eleanor Crosses', *Proceedings of the Dorset Natural History and Antiquarian Field Club*, **28** (1907), pp.209-15, esp. 213 note. Restoration efforts are described by J. Galloway, *Queen Eleanor of Castile and the Monuments Erected in her Memory* (London, 1909), and N. Smith, 'The Eleanor Cross, Geddington', *The Conservation Bulletin* (June, 1988), pp.8-10, reproduced below, p.94.

[84] G. G. Scott, *The National Memorial to the Prince Consort* (London, 1873), pp.16, 35-36. Credit for suggesting the crosses to Scott as a model for the Albert Memorial was claimed by J. Abel, *Memorials of Queen Eleanor, Illustrated by Photography: with a short account of their history and present condition* (London, 1864), unpaginated preface. I am grateful to Mr John Shrive, of Bodham House, Holt, Norfolk, for drawing this work to my attention and allowing me to inspect his copy.

[85] Pope-Hennessy, *Agnes Strickland, passim.*

[86] Strickland rarely if ever cites the edited documents in Botfield, *Manners*, pp.95-139. Her footnotes refer only to Botfield's introductory remarks, raising strong suspicions that she never actually consulted the documents themselves.

[87] K. Patmore, *The Seven Edwards of England* (London, 1911), p. 24.

[88] '*Domine camere filiarum.* Domine Ermentrude de Sakevill et aliis sex dominabus camerarum Domine [*sic*] Alienore et Margarete filiarum Regis que fuerunt de camera

Regine consortis, que annuatim capere dilectauerunt Dominum Regem in lecto suo in crastino Pasche et ipsum sic captum finire fecerunt. de dono Regis speciali licet ipsum non sic ceperunt hoc anno pro huiusmodi fine ipsius Regis de consueto viuente Regina. . . . xiiij.<u>li</u>.' (E 101/624/51, fol. 9r).

The Commissioning and Design of the Eleanor Crosses

Nicola Coldstream

The death on 28th November 1290 of Eleanor of Castile, wife of King Edward I of England, was the occasion of the most magnificent funerary display ever accorded an English monarch, let alone a consort: her memory was enshrined in no fewer than three tombs and twelve memorial crosses, spaced across eastern England from Lincoln through the east Midlands to London. Not even Prince Albert was commemorated with quite such a concentration of monuments, and an immediate and insistent question is, clearly, why? Not, why did Queen Victoria not emulate her distant ancestor on the death of a beloved spouse, but why did Edward I demand such an unprecedented memorial at the death of his? That he was grief-stricken there can be no doubt, and extreme grief can often lead to extravagant gestures, but it seems that the commemorations of Eleanor were also the culmination of an architectural and artistic programme designed to impress on the people an image and idea of the splendour of royalty.[1]

The Eleanor Crosses are, however, not simply interesting symbols. They also represent a key moment in the history of English art, one of those sudden evolutionary shifts after which nothing is quite the same again. In addition, unlike the vast majority of objects studied by medievalists, they are astonishingly well documented: we know exactly when most of them were made, and by whom; and the documents also provide valuable insights into how such a project was realised.[2]

Eleanor died at Harby, near Lincoln; after her body had been eviscerated and embalmed, her entrails were reserved for burial in Lincoln Cathedral, and the remains were conveyed in procession to London. Her heart was buried, at her request, in the church of the Dominican friars, the Blackfriars, in London, and her skeleton in Westminster Abbey. At each place that the funeral cortège stopped for the night Edward ordered a memorial cross to be set up. The stopping places were Lincoln, Grantham, Stamford, Geddington, Northampton (at Hardingstone), Stony Stratford, Woburn, Dunstable, St Albans, Waltham, West Cheap in the city of London, and the royal mews at Charing more or less on the site of the modern National Gallery and Trafalgar Square. The chronicler of Dunstable described how, after the bier had rested the night in the priory church, the cortège passed through the town, stopping in the market place while 'the king's chancellor and great men there present had marked a fitting place where they might afterwards erect, at the king's expense, a cross of wonderful size'.

The twelve crosses were made between 1291 and 1294, and three survive, at Waltham, Hardingstone and Geddington. There are fragments of the Cheapside cross in the Museum of London, and both Cheapside and Charing are known from drawings that are accurate enough at least to show their general characteristics, if not clear details. The cross now outside Charing Cross mainline station is a modern replacement. The only crosses of which there is no contemporary documentary record are those at Grantham, Stamford and Geddington, but the Geddington cross survives, as it were, in the flesh; in some ways it is stylistically the odd man out, which makes the loss of the others even more tantalising. In theory the entire funeral and its aftermath were to be paid for by Eleanor's executors from the proceeds of her estates, and it is their accounts that survive. In practice the costs, some £2000 by 1294, were so exorbitant that they had to be topped up from elsewhere. The king was, in any case, paying for other, related, works, and it may be that the costs of the undocumented crosses were absorbed into the king's accounting system: the king's works were so closely enmeshed with those of Eleanor's executors that at least one payment was made from Eleanor's estate for the bronze effigy that Edward was having made of his father, Henry III.

The surviving crosses are polygonal in plan, except for Geddington, which is triangular and indicates that there was more than one basic plan. In elevation, however, the structure is consistent. There are three receding tiers, like a wedding cake, comprising a solid base, an open tier with niches sheltering statues of the queen, and an upper solid tier, which supported the cross shaft. This is now in all cases broken off. There is some doubt about the actual termination of the shaft; it should have been a cross, but there is some evidence of a pyramidal tip, and some documents refer to a circular crown. Although the cross-bases, which are all that strictly speaking remain to us, are impressively high, the middle storey displaying the statues of the queen dominates the whole. From whichever angle you view the cross a figure of Eleanor is always in front of your eyes. There was never any doubt of her identity, as each cross was decorated with shields of the arms to which the queen was entitled, England, León, Castile and Ponthieu. The details of the ornament are as consistent as the structure. Waltham cross (illustration 2) has a number of characteristics that frequently recur. The sides of the base are each decorated with an arch-and-gable motif, with the shields of arms set in. At

56

Waltham the gables, which enclose a pointed trilobe motif and are decorated with foliage cresting, are set against a background of rosette diaper. A foliate cornice divides the base from the open storey, which itself has a small parapet of quadrilobes beneath miniature battlements. The niches sheltering the statues of the queen are deep, bordered by tall pinnacles and surmounted by gables lavishly decorated with foliage. The arch-and-gable motif is repeated in the upper tier, together with the little parapet. The polygonal plan, the deep niches and the layering of gables and finials emphasise the three-dimensionality of the cross.

At Hardingstone (illustration 3) the base has the same elements of arch-and-gable with tracery and suspended shields of arms, and every alternate face has the addition of an open book, presumably once inscribed with suitable texts. Blind tracery and foliage adorn the pinnacles as well as the gables. Here the mouldings are continuous, without capitals or bases, and there is the suggestion of a reversed, or ogee, curve, also to be seen in the niches sheltering the statues. The niches here are particularly chunky and three-dimensional, encrusted with finials and seaweedlike foliage. The cornices of the Hardingstone cross are of large leaves rather than quadrilobes or battlements, but the foliage in the gables and the plain panelling in the topmost tier immediately beneath the cross-shaft both recur on other pieces.

The last surviving cross, at Geddington (illustration 4), the royal manor not far from Northampton, is different. Although it is undocumented, there is no reason to suppose that it is not contemporary with the other crosses, and its characteristics may well have been shared by the crosses that we know nothing about, between there and Lincoln. Where Waltham and Hardingstone are polygonal, Geddington is triangular, its undulating sides formed of the so-called wave moulding that was just coming into fashion,[3] and its principal, indeed overwhelming, form of adornment is rosette diaper, of which a certain amount appears on the Waltham cross. Geddington is tall and slender, with regular rows of patterning; the shields are small and neat, the parapets reduced to simple battlements. The rosette diaper is continued in the upper pinnacles, although, like Hardingstone, the Geddington cross has foliate motifs in the niche gables.

This distinctive and consistently-applied ornament is not unique to the Eleanor crosses. In the same decade it was used in other works, some associated specifically with the queen, others not. Her only surviving tomb, in Westminster Abbey (illustration 9), is decorated with arch-and-gable motifs with continuous mouldings, inset with shields of arms. The tomb in Lincoln Cathedral, which was drawn by Dugdale,[4] seems to have been identical. Other tombs in Westminster Abbey that show strong parallels to the crosses are those of Edmund Crouchback, Earl of Lancaster, the brother of Edward I, who died in 1296, and his first wife, Aveline de Forz, who had died in 1272, but whose tomb seems to be contemporary with that of her husband. These tombs are undocumented, but only Edward could have granted permission for them, and their stylistic resemblance to the Eleanor crosses, together with the date of Crouchback's death, makes it very likely that they were made in the mid-1290s.

The sarcophagus of the Crouchback tomb (illustration 5) has the arch-and-gable, continuous mouldings, seaweed foliage and shields, and also little figures of weepers, which will be considered later (and see also Phillip Lindley's essay). The canopy is in three parts, with pinnacles, diaper, miniature battlements, seaweed foliage, overlapping gables, and blind tracery with the hint of an ogee curve that also occurs at Hardingstone. Another characteristic feature of Hardingstone appears on the coronation chair, which Edward had remade after he had stolen the Stone of Scone from Scotland: blind panels of tracery similar to those on the top tier of the Hardingstone cross.

One other work that was begun in the 1290s was the chapel of St Stephen in the Palace of Westminster (illustration 6), refounded by Edward I in 1292. St Stephen's chapel was destroyed in the fire at Westminster in 1834, but some drawings of it had been made before then, and in the immediate aftermath antiquaries did go into the smouldering ruins to try to record what was left; and the crypt, heavily restored, is still there.[5] Its building history is both complicated and lengthy, but the first campaign lasted until 1297, when Edward I stopped all works of this sort in order to finance his wars with France and Scotland. It is presumed that much of the design of St Stephen's had been drawn up and partly executed by then, and it included some of the characteristics of the Eleanor crosses, in panelling, the use of ogees in tracery, seaweed foliage in vault bosses and overlapping layers, as in the freestanding tracery bars brought down across the crypt windows.

The first master mason of St Stephen's, and therefore its designer, was Master Michael of Canterbury. It should come as no surprise to discover that he was one of the team that made the Eleanor crosses, being the mason in charge of the Cheapside cross. All the crosses of which we have record were made by one, slightly loosely formed, team of masons, closely associated with contemporary royal building works.[6] Richard of

Crundale, maker of the Charing cross, worked at Westminster Abbey and the Tower of London; all five crosses between Hardingstone and St Albans were made by John of Battle, the undermaster at Edward's foundation of Vale Royal Abbey in Cheshire. The Waltham cross was made by Roger Crundale and Dymenge de Reyns, with the help of Alexander of Abingdon, 'imaginator'; after Waltham was finished Dymenge and Alexander were despatched to work on the tomb at Lincoln; they also produced models for images on the heart tomb at Blackfriars and Alexander also made images for the Charing cross, which Roger took over after Richard Crundale died in 1293. William of Ireland also worked on the crosses for Hardingstone and Lincoln, the latter being in the charge of Richard of Stow. John of Battle had several other helpers, not always named, for the five crosses for which he was responsible.

The crosses are so similar that there must have been an overall directive, presumably issued by the King, but with the details entrusted to the designer. How far the individual makers had scope to draw up their own moulding profiles and other details is by no means clear. The different plan and use of the wave moulding at Geddington perhaps argues that they were given considerable freedom, but against that the accounts hint at a fairly strong central organisation. Much of the work for all the crosses was done in London, or at least ordered from there. There are payments for the transport of images to Hardingstone, and many of the Purbeck marble mouldings were supplied ready cut by the famous firm of Canons of Corfe, who specialised in supplying precut pieces in this very hard stone, and who must have worked to templates and patterns sent from London. The mason in charge at the London end seems to have been Richard of Crundale, at any rate until 1293. He was the maker of Charing, the most splendid cross of all. Both the London crosses outshone the others: where the average cost of the crosses outside London was about £100, Cheapside cost £226 and Charing more than £700. It seems to have taken far longer to make, and formidable quantities of expensive Purbeck marble were ordered for it. Its importance is underlined in the marginal notes to the accounts, where it is the only one to be mentioned by name. Any payment for the others (including Cheapside) has the marginal note *Crux*, but payments for Charing are signalled *Charing*. Richard of Crundale was also, like many leading master masons, a stone contractor, and it was he who organised much of the purchase and delivery of stone from Caen and from Corfe to be used on all the crosses, and he often also acted as middleman.

It is impossible now to say whether Richard was the designer in charge of the whole project. Michael of Canterbury was the designer of St Stephen's chapel, and he possibly also designed the Crouchback and de Forz tombs in Westminster Abbey, all of which have strong stylistic affinities to the Eleanor crosses. For the chapel and tombs Michael could have borrowed Richard's ideas, or he could have designed the whole lot and put Richard in charge of the crosses while he worked at St Stephen's. The question remains open.

These works, the crosses, tombs and chapel, all made or begun at the same time by the same people, seem to represent a coherent programme, which Edward I must have instituted for a deliberate purpose.[7] Crosses put up to commemorate the distinguished dead were not unknown in late 13th-century England. It was an Anglo-Saxon habit, and in the later Middle Ages there was a cross in the Strand in London which was believed to have been placed by William II in memory of his mother. Henry III had set up a cross at Merton in Surrey to commemorate the Earl of Warenne. These crosses, however, were isolated, single monuments. The true parallels to the series of Eleanor crosses are, or were, on the other side of the Channel in the kingdom of France. Louis IX had been the most glorious monarch in Europe; he died at Tunis in 1270 on the way home from Crusade, and his funeral procession from Aigues-Mortes to Paris, which took ten days to complete the journey, was marked at every overnight stopping place by a large memorial cross, known as a *montjoie*. These are now destroyed, but they are known from a drawing (where they show a close structural similarity to the Eleanor crosses, with three tiers and niches for statues of the king), and by the appearance of the cross at Lusignan in the early 15th-century *Très Riches Heures* of the Duc de Berry.[8] It is more or less certain that Edward had the *montjoies* in mind when he ordered the crosses in memory of his wife.

As with the crosses, so with the tombs. Canopied tombs of the type made for Westminster in the 1290s were only just coming into fashion in England, as were the weepers that adorned the sarcophagus. Both, however, had already been established in France, particularly to mark the burial places of royal persons and leading ecclesiastics. Louis IX had himself instituted two sets of tombs, one series at Royaumont Abbey for members of his family, and another at Saint-Denis Abbey to commemorate his royal ancestors as far back as the Merovingians,[9] and his cousins on the English throne seem to have done something similar.

Westminster Abbey was effectively rebuilt by Henry III, who took over the financing in 1245, and converted the abbey church into a huge

60

setting for the shrine of his favourite saint, Edward the Confessor.[10] He himself was buried in the Confessor's now vacant tomb (the Confessor's remains being in the shrine) after his death in 1272. There is no evidence that he intended it as a burial church for anyone other than himself and the Confessor; and it was his son Edward I who turned the saint's chapel in particular into the royal mausoleum: at Eleanor's death, Edward arranged not only for her tomb to be placed on the north side of the shrine, but also a new tomb for Henry III right opposite the shrine itself in the bay west of Eleanor's, with his own tomb west of Henry's. Not only that: he also, as we have seen, allowed the tombs of his brother Edmund Crouchback and of Aveline de Forz to be set up on the north side of the sanctuary, beside the high altar. He seems therefore to have been imitating rather closely the activities of Louis IX, appropriately, perhaps, for the man who, at the death of Louis, assumed the latter's place as leading monarch of Europe. Simple and neat though this explanation is, however, it does not fit all the available evidence. The English responded to France not by imitation but by adaptation, and Edward was not the only player on the English side.

The French policy to which the English were responding seems to be clear enough. Louis IX, who had begun his reign in 1226, thirteen years before Edward was even born, had realised that visual imagery could be used very effectively in promoting the interests of the royal house, in persuading his perhaps reluctant subjects of the sanctity and legitimacy of the monarchy. In a series of moves he had deliberately set out to stamp that image and interpretation of the French monarchy on the minds of the people. His Sainte-chapelle, attached to the royal palace in Paris, was built from 1240 as a setting for the newly acquired relic of the Crown of Thorns.[11] It is a jewelled cage of glass, sculpture and surface ornament that both glorifies the holy relic and, through the iconography of the stained glass, reflects back on the glory of the king who brought it into being. The tombs of his ancestors in the royal abbey of Saint-Denis were a perpetual reminder of the longevity and stability of the French monarchy (the latter particularly necessary, as although the French royal house had lasted unchanged for many centuries, its grip on France had been strong for only about one century); and the *montjoies*, dotted through the southern part of the kingdom which had been conquered only in the lifetime of Louis himself, were a reminder of the memory of that glorious monarch.

It was in fact Henry III, the contemporary and cousin of Louis IX, not Edward, who first caught on to the significance of Louis's patronage, and Henry who started what Edward then tried to finish. The only exact correspondence between the works of Louis and Edward is in the *montjoies*; Edward's policy towards burial in Westminster Abbey seems to combine the roles of Royaumont and Saint-Denis; and although parallels are frequently drawn between the Sainte-chapelle on the one hand and St Stephen's chapel on the other, the differences between the two are as strong as their similarities. While decoratively they may have something in common, St Stephen's was not a reliquary chapel. Henry III had been intensely jealous of the Crown of Thorns, but when he shortly afterwards acquired a relic of the Holy Blood, he put it not in a chapel of its own but in the abbey.[12] The abbey church, not St Stephen's, was the English equivalent of the Sainte-chapelle, even more so after 1297, when Louis IX was canonised and his head-reliquary placed in his chapel. At that point both Westminster Abbey and the Sainte-chapelle were the guardians of both an important holy relic and the bones of a sainted king.

Although the architecture of Westminster Abbey responds to several French churches, it also makes specific reference to the Sainte-chapelle, both in window designs and, more important, in its type and degree of interior decoration (illustration 7). The Sainte-chapelle inaugurated a type of highly burnished and encrusted interior in which colour and sculpture play a dominant part, with the use of all-over surface decoration, fake enamel, foliage, busts of angels, as well as full-size figures of the Apostles. At Westminster the entire wall surface was covered in rosette diaper which was whitewashed and picked out in gold, as a background to applied figure sculpture. This type of interior, which has great dramatic intensity, was called by Geoffrey Webb 'illuminated architecture',[13] a most apt and vivid appellation. Henry III, however, went further than adopting the function and style of the Sainte-chapelle for his royal abbey church: he also established it as the church for coronations and royal marriages, with Edward, as we have seen, adding the function of a mausoleum. Thus, by the end of the 13th century, Westminster combined in one church what in France was the function of several: burials in Saint-Denis and Royaumont, coronations at Reims Cathedral, marriages at Notre-Dame. Henry and Edward perhaps felt unable to emphasise the legitimacy of their line by commemorating their ancestors: the English royal line was, compared to that of France, subject to frequent interruptions, and the royal burials were widely scattered, in Normandy, Fontevrault on the Loire, Faversham, Reading and Winchester. They did, however, want to establish the abbey as the venue for significant royal events, in which they succeeded triumphantly, for the abbey is still the coronation church, even if its role as a marriage and funerary church is sometimes ignored.

The Eleanor crosses, then, can be seen as the culmination of a deliberate policy by Henry III and Edward I to use visual statements in the interests of the royal house. In art historical terms, however, far from being a culmination, they are literally pivotal. Heavily encrusted illuminated architecture does not seem to have caught on in France; while the architectural ideas of the Sainte-chapelle and related buildings went on to influence building designs for several generations, the French never took to the idea of decorating their interiors in this dramatic and theatrical fashion. In England things were different. The diapered and sculptured interior of Westminster provided a lead that others were to follow, notably the Angel Choir of Lincoln Cathedral, begun in 1256, again as a setting for an important relic, the body of their sainted bishop, Hugh. Not only is it a highly coloured and decorated interior, with abundant use of Purbeck marble and foliage sculpture, but the spandrels of the middle storey contain relief carvings of the angels that give the choir its name. Yet the future lay not with monumental cathedral and abbey churches, but with smaller buildings.

There is a qualitative difference between the decoration of Westminster and Lincoln and that of the Eleanor crosses and Westminster tombs, which could be put down to differences in size and function, but is actually occasioned by the nature of the decorative details employed. The decoration of the crosses and tombs, while including diaper and figure sculpture, consists to a large extent of architectural forms such as tracery, arches, gables, pinnacles and buttresses rendered on a very small scale. These are apparently new to the repertory. The origins of this stylistic phenomenon, known as micro-architecture, are to be sought in such work as canopies over statues on monumental French cathedral façades, such as Noyon Cathedral,[14] dating from about 1235. By the 1290s, however, micro-architecture had moved into many art forms, in particular precious metal reliquaries such as the destroyed shrine of St Gertrude at Nivelles, which, made in about 1270, has much in common with the Eleanor crosses: tracery, ogees, seaweed and diaper.[15] But the Eleanor crosses themselves have much in common with buildings such as St Stephen's chapel: and it is precisely this fusion of the monumental with the miniature in works of the last twenty years of the 13th century that turned English architecture on its head. In small buildings and large sculptured pieces such as the crosses and tombs the distinction between architecture and sculpture became irretrievably blurred.

The tragedy is that we have lost so many of the buildings. Of the chapels built from about 1280 to about 1330, very few survive. Lady chapels added to monastic or cathedral churches suffered particularly badly, not so much in the Reformation as in Puritan times: we have lost Lady chapels at Peterborough, Norwich and Bury St Edmunds that were, by all available evidence, magnificently decorated. We do, however, have some others. The chapel in the London residence of the bishops of Ely, now St Etheldreda's, Holborn (illustration 8), was built in 1284, a decade before St Stephen's, Westminster. Like St Stephen's, it is a small, basically plain box, but it is richly adorned with tracery, niche-work and figure sculpture.[16] The sculpture would have been brightly coloured, as were the stained-glass windows, so that the whole interior would have had a precious, jewelled effect. There were also mixed media: the effects were achieved by a combination of decorative stonework, glass and paint, a combination characteristic also of the Eleanor crosses (where little trace survives) and the Westminster tombs and St Stephen's chapel. We know from fragments and descriptions that the decorative programme of St Stephen's (admittedly dating from after 1330) included many different media, and the ornamentation of the Westminster tombs includes gilding, stucco painted to resemble marble, and glass painted to look like enamel. The great panel painting in the abbey, probably the high altar retable, and probably made c.1270, i.e. twenty years earlier, shows the same characteristics.[17]

The Westminster masons, then, were participating in a stylistic movement that celebrated the miniature and precious and specialised in a type of work that could be classed either as sculpture or as architecture. Did they invent it? Hints of their work turn up in the tomb of Archbishop Pecham (d. 1292) in Canterbury Cathedral, and both the Pecham tomb and St Etheldreda's have been attributed to Michael of Canterbury. The attribution is somewhat circular, however, because once certain buildings are ascribed to him, any other that resembles them is also said to be his. Be that as it may, the Westminster masons certainly gave the style a shove, and as a movement this miniaturist style had momentous consequences.

One aspect in particular was highly significant: the ogee curve, tentatively used on the Pecham tomb, the Eleanor crosses and the Crouchback tomb. This is its earliest known use in a monumental context in England, and its introduction transformed English architecture for a generation to come, affecting not only window tracery but the whole interior. Two surviving Lady chapels show its significance. Both are mutilated and restored, but even in their present state they are worth looking at for the hints they give of how such buildings were meant to look.[18] The Lady chapel of St Albans, finished by 1315, has a series of ogival headed niches sheltering small figures in its window embrasures; by the 1320s, when the Lady chapel at Ely was started, this tentative idea had developed into a full-scale interior design, which entirely depends on the ogee arch for its effects. It also includes the diaper work, the combination of small and large figures, foliage, overlapping layers, paint and glass that is so characteristic of the Westminster work. What transforms it as architecture is the apparent dissolution of the wall surface: although Ely is quite bulky, other buildings, such as its later contemporary, the choir of Gloucester Abbey, suggested through its surface decoration a thinning of the wall, and until the end of the Middle Ages, however thick walls were in practice, their surface decoration was designed to give an appearance of moulded fragility. This was an absolute turnaround from the heavy murality that was inherited from the Normans and prevailed until the end of the 13th century.

Equally significant are the pieces transitional between architecture and sculpture such as tombs, shrine bases and screens. These are more commensurate with the crosses themselves, and we can see the ideas at work on the shrine of St Alban,[19] and on the great pulpitum of Exeter cathedral, made c.1320, and designed by an architect and encrusted with micro-architectural ideas that turn it into a piece of monumental sculpture. All the decorative ideas here are those of the royal works of the 1290s, brought up to date, and these pieces provide the visual link to the architecture in which they are set.

So, to sum up. The Eleanor crosses are deeply significant in the history of medieval English art, for they represent the stylistic movement that transformed the church interior into a highly ornamented space and at the same time blurred the gap between architecture and sculpture, a gap that was not to be opened again before the end of the Middle Ages. They enabled Edward I to complete the programme inaugurated by his father of imposing on his subjects an image of royalty in all its splendour, but here expressed, in the statues of the queen, through elegance, grace and virtue. This is not to say that these cenotaphs and all the other extensive arrangements for Eleanor's commemoration were not also an expression of grief. Any study of Edward I reveals that he never had a single motive for his actions, and the political act would not, to him, be incompatible with a genuine expression of bereavement.[20] On a more personal note, Charing cross, the most splendid of all the crosses, was situated at Charing Mews, where Edward kept his falcons. Edward's favourite form of hunting was falconry and his falcons were much prized. He would have looked at this cross every time he went to Charing Mews. Is it too fanciful to suggest that at some deeper level Edward identified his adored wife with his favourite birds?

Acknowledgements

I am grateful to Professor George Zarnecki, the Courtauld Institute and the National Monuments Record for permission to reproduce their photographs; to David Parsons for help, encouragement and for organising the study day on which this paper was first read; and to the students present on that day, who made many valuable comments.

Notes

[1] For a full account of the making of the crosses see H. M. Colvin, ed., *The History of the King's Works*, 1: *The Middle Ages* (London, 1963), pp.479-85. See also *Age of Chivalry* (exhibition catalogue, ed. J. Alexander and P. Binski, London, Royal Academy, 1987), cat. nos. 368-79.

[2] The accounts are printed in B. Botfield, *Manners and Household Expenses of England*, ed. T. Hudson Turner, Roxburghe Club (1841). See also Colvin, *King's Works*.

[3] R. K. Morris, 'The development of later Gothic mouldings in England, c.1250-1400 - Part 1', *Architectural History*, 21 (1978), p.27.

[4] Illustrated in Colvin, *King's Works*, 1, pl. 35B, and *Age of Chivalry*, cat. no. 379.

[5] St. Stephen's has been discussed most recently in C. Wilson, *The Gothic Cathedral* (London, 1990), pp. 192-6; it is discussed and illustrated in *Age of Chivalry*, cat. nos. 324-5; in J. Bony, *The English Decorated Style* (Oxford, 1979), passim and pls.129-31, 277-9, 329-30; in Colvin, *King's Works*, 1, pp.510-27, pls.31-3.

[6] For the individual masons see Botfield, and for details of their careers see J. Harvey, *English Medieval Architects*, rev. ed. (Gloucester, 1984).

[7] For what follows see Colvin, *King's Works*, 1, pp.479-85; Bony, *Decorated Style*, chapters 2 and 3; L. Stone, *Sculpture in Britain: the Middle Ages*, 2nd ed. (Harmondsworth, 1972), pp.142-6.

[8] Chantilly, Musée Condé, f. 3v.

[9] See W. Sauerlaender, *Gothic Sculpture in France 1140-1270* (London, 1972), pls.272-3; A. Erlande-Brandenburg, *Le Roi est mort: étude sur les funérailles, les sépultures et les tombeaux des rois de France jusqu' à la fin du XIIIe siècle* (Paris and Geneva, 1975).

[10] For a recent discussion of Henry's and Edward's motives, including an exhaustive bibliography, see P. Binski, 'The Cosmati at Westminster and the English Court Style', *Art Bulletin*, 72.1 (1990), pp.6-34.

[11] R. Branner, *St. Louis and the Court Style* (London, 1965), pp.56-65.

[12] M. Roberts, 'The Relic of the Holy Blood and the Iconography of the Thirteenth-century North Transept Portal of Westminster Abbey', in W. M. Ormrod, ed., *England in the Thirteenth Century*, Proceedings of the 1984 Harlaxton Symposium (Grantham, 1985), pp.129-42.

[13] G. Webb, *Architecture in Britain: the Middle Ages*, 2nd ed. (Harmondsworth, 1965), p.135.

[14] Wilson, *The Gothic Cathedral*, pl.142.

[15] G. Donnay-Rocmans, 'La Châsse de Sainte Gertrude à Nivelles', *Gazette des Beaux-Arts*, **58** (1961), pp.185ff.

[16] Bony, *English Decorated Style*, pls.63-4, 66-7.

[17] P. Binski, *The Painted Chamber at Westminster*, Society of Antiquaries Occasional Papers, new series, **9** (London, 1986), pp.56-63.

[18] N. Coldstream, 'The Lady Chapel at Ely: its place in the English Decorated Style', *East Anglian and other studies presented to Barbara Dodwell*, Reading Medieval Studies, **11** (1985), pp.1-30; N. Coldstream, 'The Kingdom of Heaven: its architectural setting', in *Age of Chivalry*, pp.92-7.

[19] Bony, *English Decorated Style*, pl. 110.

[20] M. Prestwich, *Edward I* (London, 1988); but see also E. L. G. Stones, *Edward I* (Oxford, 1968).

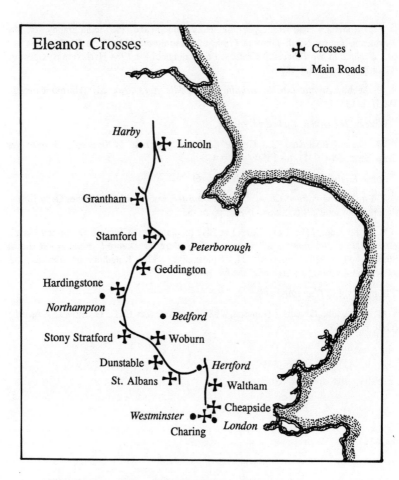

Eleanor Crosses

Crosses
Main Roads

Harby
Lincoln
Grantham
Stamford
Peterborough
Geddington
Hardingstone
Northampton
Bedford
Stony Stratford
Woburn
Dunstable
Hertford
St. Albans
Waltham
Cheapside
Westminster
London
Charing

1   **Map showing sites of the Eleanor crosses**
Martin Smith

Romanticizing Reality:
The Sculptural Memorials of Queen Eleanor and their Context

Phillip Lindley

The sculptural images of Queen Eleanor are amongst the most famous works of English medieval art. Their apparent familiarity, though, is a little illusory: scant attention has been paid to stylistic variation within individual monuments, a problem which recent conservation work on the sculptures has highlighted. Inevitably, any reconsideration of these figures must also entail a brief look at related imagery and this essay will accordingly be divided into three sections. The first part will examine the gilt-bronze effigy of Queen Eleanor on her tomb in Westminster Abbey and the context in which this image should be seen. The second section will survey the freestone images of the queen from the three surviving Eleanor crosses, those at Hardingstone, Geddington and Waltham. Recent conservation work on the first two crosses, and the conservation of one of the images from that at Waltham, makes it possible to reassess their sculptural styles and their relationship with the Westminster effigy. Finally, the naming of two of the sculptors in the extant documentary evidence provides an unusual opportunity to examine the place of individual artists' works within the context of late thirteenth-century sculpture. This period saw an intense experimentation in the style, iconography and deployment of sculpture, paralleling - and, indeed, forming a significant part of - the developments in architecture which propelled England into the vanguard of European art.[1]

(I) The gilt-bronze effigies of Queen Eleanor of Castile in Westminster Abbey and Lincoln Cathedral, and the heart burial at the London Blackfriars

Queen Eleanor of Castile died at Harby in Nottinghamshire on 28 November 1290. The queen's corpse was first taken to Lincoln, where it was eviscerated; the corpse and heart were then brought to London while the bowels were separately buried at Lincoln Cathedral. A separate monument was provided at each of these locations and the sites at which her funeral cortège halted en route to Westminster Abbey were marked by a cross featuring freestone images of the queen. These crosses, then, form an important component of a monumental programme of a scope and splendour which is uniquely ambitious in the history of the English monarchy.[2] The practice of burying the entrails or heart separately from the rest of the corpse was not uncommon at the time, in spite of papal disapproval of the practice, but it was still exceptional to have three separate tombs, for the heart, bowels and corpse. Many medieval monuments have invocations to the viewer to pray for the deceased, thus assisting the departed soul through Purgatory, and the underlying motive for providing three tombs and the memorial crosses, apart from the potential for lavish secular display which they provided, was to maximise the number of prayers for Eleanor's soul.[3] The pages of the books carved on the lower stage of the Hardingstone cross were doubtless painted with requests to the viewers to pray for the deceased queen.

Eleanor's two principal tombs were those for her body in Westminster Abbey (illustration 9) and for her bowels in Lincoln Cathedral. Henry III's rebuilding of the abbey church from 1245 had made that building a worthy rival to King Louis IX's Sainte-Chapelle in Paris, or Amiens and Rheims cathedrals, which were rebuilt in the early thirteenth century.[4] Henry himself had wished to be buried in the abbey and may have prepared the Cosmati tomb on the north side of Edward the Confessor's chapel, flanking the Confessor's shrine (made by the same workmen and probably completed in 1269, just three years before his death).[5] It is possible that it was Henry's intention to found in the abbey a dynastic mausoleum to rival Saint-Denis, where, in 1263-4, sixteen effigies of Louis IX's Carolingian and Capetian ancestors had been commissioned.[6] However, it was under Henry's son, Edward I (and his successors), that the project actually developed. It never, though, possessed the same retrospective accent that St. Louis's programme exhibited, for two principal reasons. First, the English monarchy could pretend to nothing like the genealogical continuity of the French royalty; moreover, many of the earlier English kings had been buried at their own foundations or at Winchester. Secondly, as Henry III was well aware, the shrine of Edward the Confessor at Westminster itself provided a devotional and political asset which the Capetians were unable to match until Louis IX was himself canonised in 1297.[7]

In 1291, Edward commissioned William Torel, a London goldsmith, to cast *three* life-size gilt-bronze effigies: one of Henry III (illustration 12), to be placed on top of the king's Italianate Cosmatesque tomb, and two apparently identical effigies of Eleanor of Castile.[8] One was intended for the tomb chest in the abbey (illustrations 10 and 11), while the duplicate was destined to lie on the tomb over Eleanor's entrails at Lincoln.

Cathedral. The first point to make about the gilt-bronze effigy of Queen Eleanor in Westminster Abbey, therefore, is that it should be seen in the context of the larger commission for three effigies. It seems unlikely that Edward had intended before his consort's death to commemorate his father with a gilt-bronze effigy, because the Cosmati-work base is too tall for it to be possible to see the figure properly.[9]

Eleanor's heart was brought to the Dominican church in London where the heart of her son Alphonso was also buried.[10] The heart-tomb in the Blackfriars was destroyed before any visual record was made of it, but, judging from documentary evidence, it was a smaller monument, featuring as many as three metal images, made by William of Suffolk, and a figure of an angel holding a representation of the queen's heart for which Adam the Goldsmith was paid ten marks: master Walter of Durham and Alexander of Abingdon were involved in the decorations round the heart-burial tomb in 1291-2, which stood in a chapel, possibly the Lady Chapel on the north side of the choir.[11] In its small scale and metalwork images, this monument must have perfectly represented the intersection between goldsmiths' work, architecture and sculpture which is so remarkable a feature of the Decorated style.

William Torel's three life-size figures were probably the first three-dimensional bronze effigies on such a scale in medieval England. There was, it is true, some precedent for the provision of cast-bronze tomb effigies in this country and in the middle of the thirteenth century three bishops seem to have been commemorated with effigies of the low-relief type which can still be seen in Bishop Everard de Fouilloy's (d.1222) figure at Amiens.[12] It may have been an effigy of this sort that Henry III or his artistic adviser had in mind when in 1257 a skilled sculptor called Master Simon was called to Westminster from Wells to make a tomb for the king's deaf and dumb daughter, Katherine, who had died in infancy.[13] Master Simon appears to have been planning to cast a three-dimensional figure; the treasurer was ordered to pay him eighty marks in instalments for his work on an image in gilt bronze for the princess's tomb, but Simon may have been unable to overcome the technical difficulties of casting the effigy: six weeks later five and a half marks were paid to Master Simon of Wells 'who should have made a bronze image over the tomb of Katherine, the king's daughter'.[14] The alternative explanation for Simon's dismissal, namely that Henry decided to commission an even more splendid monument from the goldsmith, William of Gloucester - who made an effigy consisting of a wooden core covered with silver-gilt plates and decorated with pearls and amethysts - seems unsatisfactory in view of the

71

fact that its total cost, £35 11s. 0d., was less than that set aside for Simon's cast-bronze effigy.[15] William of Gloucester's effigy of Katherine has itself disappeared, but some indication of its possible construction is derived from the effigy of Henry III's half-brother, William de Valence (d.1296), which was imported from Limoges and is made of metal plates and enamels nailed to a wooden core.[16.]

It is unlikely that Torel had ever before been asked to cast images of such a size, given both the lack of precedents for such effigies and the considerable and unnecessary thickness of the castings (rendering them both extremely heavy and very expensive).[17] He seems to have set himself up in a shed in the abbey churchyard,[18] and spent the next two years on the project. The original models were probably made of wax, as is revealed by the references in the accounts to the carrying of large quantities of the material from his house to the workshop, to form the images.[19] Metal was purchased from two English merchants, and a quantity of gold florins was bought from Lucchese merchants for the gilding.[20] The Westminster effigy was completed first and by spring 1293 was placed on its marble tomb, made by Richard of Crundale.[21] Queen Eleanor's tomb at Lincoln Cathedral was destroyed during the Commonwealth period, but fortunately a representation of it survives in Sir William Dugdale's *Book of Monuments*.[22] This depiction shows that the Lincoln image, which was cast early in 1293, was probably identical to that at Westminster; presumably it was cast from the same mother-mould.

The Westminster effigy (illustration 11) was protected by a wooden cover, or tester, now lost, painted in 1293 by Master Walter of Durham (who also painted that of Henry III) and, towards the ambulatory, by the surviving iron grille with eleven panels of scrolled foliage and terminating in a *chevaux-de-frise*, wrought by Master Thomas of Leighton at a cost of £12.[23] The sides of the Purbeck marble tomb-chest are divided into six bays of trefoil-headed arches under crocketed gables with quatrefoils in the heads, and diagonally-turned pinnacles. Shields of arms (England, Leon and Castile and Ponthieu) suspended from foliage are housed under the arches: in the nineteenth century, gilding could still be seen on some of the mouldings.[24] The sub-base, towards the ambulatory, was decorated with painting also by Walter of Durham and the damaged remains of this work seem to show a representation of Edward I's Savoyard counsellor Sir Otto de Grandson praying to the Virgin to intercede on behalf of Eleanor's soul, with four hooded mourners to the left of the painted sepulchre behind him. It is possible that Queen Eleanor, flanked by the Crucifixion and saints Thomas and Edmund (?) (all housed under separate architectural

72

canopies reminiscent of those in the stained glass of Merton College, Oxford) was also shown in a tile pavement in the aisle below the tomb.[25] The effigy, with the pair of cushions at the head and the two lions at her feet, was cast in a single piece, but for the right hand which was made separately and then fixed to the figure.[26] The cushions were elaborately chased with the arms of Leon and Castile and enamels or paste jewels were attached by small pins to the clothing and crown; only the sockets remain (illustration 10).[27]

It has been suggested that Eleanor's splendid effigy, which can be related stylistically to figures in less precious materials, may have been derived from the representation of her on her seal (which Lethaby, indeed, plausibly attributes to Torel).[28] There is no persuasive reason to view this as a direct source. Although the gable over the queen's head is not dissimilar to that shown on the seal, the effigy canopy originally possessed side-shafts, and the gable is, in any case, a familiar component of freestone or marble tomb effigies.[29] What has happened here is that a format suited to exterior sculptures has been brought inside the building and laid flat on its back: the architectural details have no structural role, but are employed decoratively. There is, then, a tension (which is common in English Gothic tomb sculpture) between the actual recumbency of the effigy and the verticality which is implied by the use of a niche and by the handling of the draperies.[30] This contradiction is highlighted by the fact that although her head rests on a pair of cushions, Queen Eleanor is shown with her eyes open and holding the fastening of her cloak. It is, in fact, very rare in thirteenth-century England, and indeed the rest of Northern Europe, to find an effigy with the eyes closed as if dead; there are some examples, most notably in the well-known retrospective effigies of Saxon bishops at Wells Cathedral, or the figure of a priest at Little Steeping in Lincolnshire, but these are very uncommon.[31]

The effigy of Queen Eleanor does not constitute a deliberate portrait of the queen in the modern sense: although thirteenth-century sculptors were, to judge by some of the results, copying from life, there does not yet seem to have been an active desire for realistic portraiture, untempered by idealisation, in tomb effigies. In general we have to wait until the fourteenth century for such concerns to become important.[32] This is essentially an idealised image of the queen, one which is virtually interchangeable with representations of saints or of the Virgin Mary.[33] It should be remarked in this context that the effigy of King Henry III (illustration 12), which has been claimed as a genuine portrait of the king, must also be rejected on the same grounds, although the additional objection can be raised that Henry died two decades before the effigy was cast.[34]

Recent commentators have rather downplayed the stylistic importance of Queen Eleanor's effigy; this is partly because works which more probably post-date the figure have been misdated to an earlier period, and have therefore been seen as models.[35] The elegant modelling of the draperies, the sinuous lines of the edges of the cloak, the calm idealising of the head, and the dignified suavity of the gently swaying figure, provided one potent source of inspiration for the weepers on the tomb of Edmund Crouchback (d.1296).[36] The manner in which the queen fingers the ribbon of her cloak is a motif familiar from the statuary of the west front of Wells Cathedral, dating from the first half of the thirteenth century, and is repeated in Queen Eleanor's seal:[37] but the comparison with Wells serves rather to demonstrate the profound disjunction between works of the first half of the century and this image. The fluidity and plasticity of the modelling are far removed from the wooden and rather static feel of even the best Wells imagery. Undoubtedly, the sculptural works of Henry III at Westminster Abbey and the later work at Lincoln Cathedral form important intermediate stages in the development towards the figure style of the effigy.[38]

The effigy of King Henry III is an equally remarkable figure, possessing the same powerfully idealised quality, but with scooped V-shaped folds troughed over the stomach and framed by the hands which once bore sceptres, arranged on subtly varying diagonals.[39] The king's mantle, fastened by a brooch on his right shoulder,[40] falls in shallow, sinuous curves which paradoxically serve to emphasise the monumentality of the figure with its profound and sensitive head (illustration 12). Again its innovations were taken up in the weepers of Crouchback's tomb.[41] Thanks to their stylistic and technical merits, the figures of Henry and Eleanor are amongst the most successful of all medieval tomb-effigies, combining the idealising preoccupations of the mid-thirteenth century with the fluidity of movement and grace which was characteristic of the early fourteenth century.[42] In the next section we have to see how far the sculptures of Queen Eleanor on the three surviving crosses relate to Torel's effigies.

(II) The Images of Queen Eleanor at Waltham, Hardingstone and Geddington

The Westminster and Lincoln tombs with their gilt-bronze effigies of Queen Eleanor by William Torel and the heart-tomb at the London Blackfriars were the most splendid of Edward I's lavish memorial

74

arrangements for the queen. But even more important, in terms of the diffusion of new stylistic ideas, was the series of memorial crosses at the resting places of her funeral bier between Harby and Westminster (an idea imitated from the memorial crosses of Philip II (d.1223) and the *montjoies* of St. Louis).[43] Dr. Coldstream has discussed these crosses elsewhere in the volume and all that need be recalled here is that only three survive in reasonable condition.[44] The first to consider is the hexagonal, three-tiered cross at Waltham, designed by Roger of Crundale. This featured three figures of Queen Eleanor carved from high-quality imported Caen stone in 1291-2 by a sculptor who is named in the executors' accounts as one Alexander of Abingdon.[45] The figures, which are about 180 centimetres high, have been placed on loan at the Victoria and Albert Museum (two are currently inaccessible and these comments therefore generally only apply to one figure).[46] Alexander is also documented as having carved the lost images of the most important and expensive Eleanor cross, that at Charing, which was designed by the senior royal mason, Richard of Crundale.[47] Indeed all of Alexander's earliest documented works - he collaborated on the Purbeck marble tomb-chest for Queen Eleanor's viscera in Lincoln Cathedral and worked on the heart-tomb in the London Blackfriars, as well as the Waltham and Charing cross figures - are connected with Eleanor's funerary programme, and these were monuments of such prestige and importance that he must already have been a sculptor of considerable repute. It is possible, given the fact that he also worked in marble, that he carved the marble fragments which are all that remain of the second most expensive of the Eleanor crosses, that at Cheapside.[48] The use of such an expensive material, and one which would hardly seem suitable for an outdoor location, goes some way to explain the great cost of the London crosses, which were evidently intended to be the finest in the series. Works of this importance, undoubtedly testifying to Alexander's position as the best available sculptor then working in England, will have helped to make him the most influential sculptor of his generation.

Alexander's style, in so far as it can be recovered from the rather weathered statues from the Waltham cross (illustration 16), appears to be intimately linked with that of Torel's effigies at Westminster, and is even more closely paralleled in the work of the manuscript illuminator known as the 'Madonna Master' in the de Lisle Psalter (BL Arundel MS 83 part ii).[49] These illuminations give a good idea of what the Eleanor statues must have looked like when they were fully painted; it is often forgotten that the crosses and their images were highly painted and that the loss of this surface has not only made them that much more vulnerable to the weather and atmospheric pollution, but has also irretrievably impaired their aesthetic impact. A sculptural parallel to Alexander's 'Eleanors' can be seen in the weepers of Edmund Crouchback's (d.1296) tomb in Westminster Abbey: these retain most of their painted surfaces.[50] It has been persuasively argued by Lawrence Stone that Alexander was responsible for both the effigy and some (at least) of the weepers of Crouchback's monument.[51] The Waltham figures are also close in style to that of the gilt-bronze effigy of Queen Eleanor: it is true that the fluttering and rippling draperies of the best known Waltham image are not exhibited by the bronze effigy, but some allowance has to be made for the difficulties of the medium (and one of the Waltham figures, in so far as it can be judged from rather poor photographs, seems even closer to Torel's image, though the drapery is thicker).[52] What is interesting is that there are a number of features which recur; the proportions of the elegant figures, the poses, and the manner in which the draperies bend at the feet are quite close. The fact that the effigy of Henry III is even closer in style to some of the Crouchback weepers strongly reinforces these inter-connections. Alexander supplied wax models for the three metal images cast by William of Suffolk for the tomb of Queen Eleanor's heart in the London Blackfriars,[53] and it is possible that a model by him also lies behind Torel's Westminster and Lincoln effigies.

The Waltham queens reveal, in their elegantly swaying poses, subtle draperies and their calm aristocratic heads, an idealised and restrained style which is generally described as a marked contrast to the nervously fluttering draperies and taller proportions of the surviving Hardingstone cross figures (illustrations 13-15), all of which have, regrettably, been replaced on the cross after their recent conservation.[54] The Hardingstone cross, one of five designed by John of Battle, is an experiment in luxuriant undulating ornament, of cusped ogee arches, pierced fretwork and crocketed gables containing a bewildering variety of foliage types and with bulging foliate finials. The sculptor of the four images of Queen Eleanor is named in the accounts as William of Ireland. The nervous and restless style of two of the images (illustration 15), a harbinger of sculptural styles in the early fourteenth century, is a perfect complement to the cross's architecture and is admirably described by Lawrence Stone: the 'drapery hangs in sagging loops and tight little folds with tubular voluted ends', the body is covered with scooped folds and rippling hems, the cloak caught up over the left arm to provide elegant and fluttering contours.[55] There are notable differences even between these two figures: the width of the crown's brim varies considerably, and one of the queens is veiled, while the other is not; the shallow curves of the draperies on the upper torso of

76

one find no parallel in the second (it should be noted that this area appears to have been 'pieced in', presumably during Blore's restoration of the cross, and the detail looks entirely inauthentic) and the marked *déhanchement* of one figure contrasts with the rather more upright stance of the other. Examination of the second pair of images (illustrations 13 and 14) suggests that the contrast between William's style and that of Alexander of Abingdon may have been overstressed. One of the queens (illustration 13) has her cloak tucked under her left arm, like the two previous figures, and again tugged (her hand is lost) the fastening of her cloak, but instead of the scooped, sagging folds over the stomach, the rippling folds of her cloak at the side now contrast with the vertical pleats of her dress, which form deep vertical ridges (the surfaces are unfortunately much damaged) from her knees to her feet. The cloak of the remaining figure (illustration 14) is fastened with a brooch, and her left hand, down at her side, now grasps her cloak, the swaying pose accentuated by the forward thrust of the right knee and the gentle curve of the body, as if this were an ivory carving on a gigantic scale. The oval heads of all the figures, where they are well preserved, have long wavy hair, almond-shaped eyes and smiles playing on the lips.

The first of the two calmly draped figures, in particular, is close to the refined and elegant Waltham cross queen: the motif of the queen holding her cloak ribbon with her left hand, the cloak bunched up at her elbow, and the contrast between the vertical ridges of the dress folds, curving down to the feet and the busy handling of the cloak hems are all close to Alexander's Waltham figure. Nevertheless, the bodies of William's queens are taller and less well articulated than in the work of Alexander or Torel, and the quality of conception is less elevated and refined. It is these factors that have doubtless led Lawrence Stone to declare that 'it is obvious that the sculptor of the statues, William of Ireland, was not a court artist'.[56] There has been some debate recently about whether the notion of a 'court style' in this period has any real validity and there seems little doubt that if William, whose images like Alexander's were carved from imported Caen stone, and who also was based in London (whence his statues were brought to Northampton by William of Barnack),[57] is to be excluded from the status of 'court artist' then the term's usefulness is seriously undermined. The implication of such an exclusion is that only the calm and elegant styles of Alexander and Torel merit description as court art. However, the evidence of the Eleanor crosses unequivocally proves that a variety of different styles was patronised by king and court. Within the general format for the images of the queen, there was also, evidently, plenty of room for individual stylistic expression: Alexander's Waltham images exhibit a considerable variety in their handling and so do William of Ireland's Hardingstone queens. Nor, it should be recalled, are William Torel's two Westminster effigies stylistically uniform. Far too much weight has been attached to the contrast between the only currently accessible Waltham queen and a single figure from the Hardingstone cross. If photographs of the other Waltham queens had been available, or if different images from the Hardingstone cross had been selected for comparison, the contrast would have been much less dramatic.[58] Individual sculptors, it is evident, had a greater creative range than some scholars have been prepared to allow. William was paid at exactly the same rate for his statues as Alexander (five marks each)[59] and, as we shall see, it is not impossible that they actually collaborated on some works.

There are no accounts for the third surviving cross, that at Geddington.[60] Like the other crosses, it looks like the translation into stone of a piece of metalwork. Unlike them, it is triangular in shape, the lower tier entirely covered with rich diaper patterns which even spread onto the buttresses.[61] The images are placed in the second tier of the cross (illustration 17), which is not visually recessed from the first stage, as was the case at Hardingstone and Waltham. The niches, like the cross, are triangular in plan, with the angle buttress of the lower stage standing in front of the niche, effectively masking any frontal view of the statues. It is as if the architect was using the spectator's desire to see the figures to force him to move round the cross. Stylistically, the figures, which seem to be carved from a local limestone, are coarser and less accomplished than the works of Alexander or William. All three of them feature the now familiar motif which has the queen tinkering with her cloak fastening (the wrists being notably boneless), and have smiling faces whose details are obscured by the sulphation of the stone (illustration 18);[62] interestingly, all these figures show the queen's hair veiled. The first of the figures has dragged her cloak across her body with her left hand, whilst simultaneously tucking its left side under her elbow; this provides an opportunity to explore the effects of falling cloth, though the treatment of the rolls and undulations is simple and repetitive. A second figure has a drastically simpler treatment, with cloak and dress falling in straight vertical folds, bent only at the ankles. The third figure represents a stage of drapery treatment in between that of the first two images: the right side of her cloak drops in simple vertical pleats to the ground, but the left hand side is swept up under her arm, producing v-folds over the stomach and below the left elbow, with convoluted hemline rolls like those exhibited by the first figure. In every case the right arm, which stood proud of the main

78

body of the figure, is lost; protruding lumps of stone visible on the veils are all that remain of the sceptres. In general, these images exhibit little of that sensitivity towards the fall of draperies exhibited by Alexander's and William's images, and the usual criticism of them as less high quality figures seems unanswerable.

This admittedly cursory examination of the Eleanor cross figures reveals that the stylistic range of the sculptures was no less remarkable than that of the architecture. The two series of images from Hardingstone and Waltham are more closely related to one another than is generally assumed, and these products of London workshops stand at some distance from the Geddington cross figures. In the final section of this paper, an attempt will be made to establish the place of these figures in the dramatic period of change in the late thirteenth century, when the increased naturalism of the 1280s started to change in the direction of a new sinuosity and suppleness, developments which resulted in that sense of rustling, restless mobility which pervades early fourteenth-century imagery.

(III) The sculptural context of the images of Queen Eleanor

During the thirteenth century, the production of sculpted imagery increasingly became the province not of monastic craftsmen but of specialist lay sculptors, travelling from commission to commission.[63] By 1226 one 'Thomas the Imager' is already mentioned in London records and workmen are increasingly known by name from the records of work for the crown.[64] There are few instances, however, in this still scanty documentation where one can unequivocally connect a surviving image with a sculptor named in the accounts. Perhaps the first major images for which the identity of the sculptor seems secure are the remarkable Gabriel and Virgin inside the chapter house of Westminster Abbey, carved by William of Yxeworth for 53s. 4d. in 1253 and reinstated by Sir George Gilbert Scott during his restoration of the chapter house.[65] The thin, vertically pleated draperies look back to the first great sculptural programme of the early thirteenth century, the west front of Wells, but the exaggerated poses and the subtlety of modelling show a movement away from this style, and in the exploration of these new directions in sculpture Yxeworth must have played an important part.[66] This distinctive and mannered style is taken up in the Judgement portal at Lincoln Cathedral which must be the work of sculptors who had come from Westminster.[67] However, some of the porch sculpture marks a move in a different stylistic direction and by the time that the figures from the Angel Choir at Lincoln

Cathedral were being carved, some time in the 1260s or 70s, a new drapery style was increasingly in evidence, with large broad-fold garments, and crumpled heavy draperies which are strongly plastic.[68] This marked a decisive turn away from the sharp-edged, nervous and narrow pleating of Henry III's work at Westminster Abbey.

For architectural and sculptural historians, there is a certain symbolism in the placing of Queen Eleanor's viscera-tomb in the recently completed Angel Choir, for it illustrates the temporary passing of artistic initiative to the teams of artists assembled by Edward I at Westminster. Here, a whole series of developments took place, which suddenly, and for the first time, placed England in the front rank of architectural and sculptural innovation in Europe. Although some of the chief monuments of this period - the palatine chapel of St. Stephen at Westminster (illustration 6) for instance - have been destroyed or very severely altered, some of the qualities which they featured are exemplified in the tomb of Edmund Crouchback, Earl of Lancaster (d.1296) (illustration 5).[69] The combination of painted and sculpted work (the basement is painted with small soldiers), the texturing of surfaces in gesso, the imitation of an expensive medium in a cheaper one (the pinnacles featured painted glass duplicating the effects of enamelwork),[70] and the complexity and sophistication of the polychromy, are all characteristic of the Decorated style. Architecturally, Crouchback's tomb represents an important trend in the style, in employing motifs and ideas which had earlier been current in French buildings, and transforming them into a 'micro-architecture', where all the details appear on a tiny scale, although there must, surely, be some more profound meaning in the use of what is in essence a portal design for the triple canopy of a tomb.[71] Edmund's wife, Aveline, died in 1273, but her tomb appears to date from only a little earlier than that of her husband, and almost certainly postdates that of Queen Eleanor of Castile.[72] It consists of a gabled canopy with cusped arch supported on shafts and flanked by buttresses, surmounting a tomb-chest with a gabled arcade containing weepers. This is similar to, but more complex than, Eleanor's tomb-chest, where the arcade contains shields; in Aveline's tomb-chest, they were painted in the spandrels of the gables. The pinnacles are no longer turned at an angle, though they have the same two-tier format, the lower section having a trefoil head under a gable, in the head of which is a trefoil. The gabled arcade is very similar to that of Eleanor's tomb-chest, but the inner arch bases and capitals and the outer arch capitals are omitted.[73] The finials of the gables and the pinnacles are carefully integrated into the foliage-studded moulding at the top of the chest. Crouchback's tomb is even more elaborate, using three arches, the centre one wider than those flanking it. Ogee arches appear in a tentative way, and other novel features are the brackets sprouting from the central pediment upon which once stood little angels bearing candles: they can still be seen in the sixteenth-century Islip Roll.[74] In the middle of the central pediment is a trilobed panel filled with a relief of the earl praying on horseback, probably based on contemporary seal designs.[75]

The two effigies of the earl and countess are executed in a freer style than those of Henry III and Queen Eleanor, since they were carved in freestone and had none of the limitations imposed by the medium of bronze. The dynamism of the drapery handling of Aveline's effigy, and the convoluted folds of the cloak evoke the stylistic features of two of William of Ireland's Hardingstone figures. The effigy of the countess has an elaborately complicated drapery treatment, scooped out into v-folds over the stomach, the mantle's shallow, swirling hems originally enhanced by the colour contrast of the lining.[76] The weepers of these monuments are amongst the earliest in English tomb-sculpture;[77] the slightly squat appearance of the Aveline figures is partly due to the clothing worn by the images but those of Crouchback's tomb 'combine the classic dignity of the thirteenth century with the grace and mobility of the early fourteenth century'.[78] Some of them are near to the style of Alexander of Abingdon's Waltham cross queen, but others are closer to the Hardingstone Eleanors.[79] Clearly, the stylistic features of the sculpture, the importance of which is not disputed, depend directly on the images of the Eleanor crosses.

There is no documentary evidence naming the sculptors or other artists responsible for the two Westminster tombs, but it is far from impossible that Alexander and William of Ireland worked side by side at Westminster, possibly even on the same monuments. Such a hypothosis might account for the elaborately furled draperies of the Aveline effigy, which could be interpreted as a response by Alexander to William of Ireland's work.[80] Clearly, both men had their workshops in London in the early 1290s, and, equally clearly, their selection for Eleanor's memorials indicates that they were leading sculptors of their day. William Torel's exact role in the conception of his gilt-bronze effigies, whose stylistic significance I have stressed, remains tantalisingly unclear without the detailed contracts which would clarify the responsibilities of individual artists in what were, almost inevitably, collaborative projects.[81] No such doubts, however, can be attached to the place of Alexander and William. Alexander of Abingdon seems to have been the senior man: his role within the Eleanor memorials is wider and more exalted than that of William of

Ireland, who must, nevertheless, have been an important 'court artist'. The appearance of images by such sculptors on the Eleanor crosses must have been a key factor in the dissemination of metropolitan styles to the provinces. The new tastes for rhythmical surface articulation, for the undulation of line and for mobile figure-styles in the first two decades of the fourteenth century and the heightened perception of the architectonic and iconographic possibilities of figure-sculpture testify to the strength and popularity of their stylistic ideals.[82]

(IV) *Conclusions*

This general discussion of the images of Queen Eleanor has attempted to assess their place and significance within the context of late thirteenth-century sculpture. It is clear, though, that a study of this type ought to raise a number of important questions, of a sort which art-historians are just beginning to pose: questions which may, in a medium such as sculpture, where so much of the physical evidence has been destroyed through iconoclasm or neglect, be impossible to answer satisfactorily. But casting light on the roles of individuals such as Alexander or William inevitably serves to emphasise our ignorance of other sculptors of the period, and even more of the actual mechanisms at work in stylistic change. How individuals' styles were formed, the kind of training they received, the perception of stylistic change by patrons and artists, the nature of collaboration in thirteenth-century sculpture, as well as the important question whether specialised image-workers could even have existed outside London:[83] these are problems which must be addressed in the future if we are really to understand these sculptures.

Professor Parsons's essay contributes a great deal to the clarification of the historical figure of Queen Eleanor of Castile. For the art-historian, however, her physical images, images which may well have contributed as much to our view of the queen as the *Opus Chronicorum*,[84] remain rather elusive. Their place within a taxonomic system of stylistic development is by now fairly refined, because a good deal of attention has been devoted to purely formalist analysis of the sculptures. But a further attempt has been made to examine the ideological background to the huge funerary programme of which they are a part. It is still unclear why exactly Edward initiated this programme. What message were these monuments intended to convey?

As Dr. Coldstream has justly observed, the commemorations of the queen were 'designed to impress on the people an image and idea of the splendour of royalty'. But perhaps they also went beyond this. The tombs and crosses have a role which transcends the purely secular. The chantry function of the three tombs was apparently carried over into the crosses. The Dunstable chronicler relates how when the funeral procession came to his town the bier was stopped in the market place and the chancellor, assisted by nobles, chose the site where afterwards the cross was to be erected, the prior of the convent sprinkling the ground with holy water.[85] Moreover, William Rishanger, the St. Alban's chronicler, writes that the purpose of these crosses was the stimulation of prayers for the good of the queen's soul.[86] However, there is little doubt that this was not their sole function. Each cross contains several images of the queen, a multiplication of a secular figure on a scale previously unknown in this country.[87] One thing that Edward had learnt from his father was an appreciation of the propagandistic possibilities of art, although he combined its employment with a military and political skill which Henry III had almost wholly lacked. These vertical images of Queen Eleanor can be viewed as tending to elide the secular with the ecclesiastical sphere, although this is not to say that Edward *explicitly* intended any confusion between the image of a female saint and that of his deceased queen. The main tombs' positioning close to the shrines of St. Hugh and St. Edward the Confessor, the heart-tomb in the Dominican Blackfriars to which the queen herself had been a generous donor, and the chantry associations of the crosses, all can be seen as part of a programme of works designed not only to stimulate prayers for the queen but also to associate the English monarchy with spiritual authority.[88] This emphasis is in no sense, of course, at odds with Edward's employment of historical and genealogical materials and iconography to consolidate the authority of his kingship. By the multiplication and geographical distribution of images of Queen Eleanor, Edward influenced the public view of her, distancing the idealised figure from the unpleasantly acquisitive, land-hungry historical reality. What his programme of monuments also did, of course, was to turn her, in effect, into a figure from a romance of the kind which both he and Eleanor read, and which he employed successfully elsewhere to buttress his power.[89] It is a tribute to the king's success that the sculptural images of Eleanor of Castile have so powerfully influenced the historical perception of the queen.

Acknowledgements

The author is indebted to the British Academy for the Post-doctoral Research Fellowship during the tenure of which this paper was written, and to Paul Williamson, John Parsons, Christopher Norton and Paul Crossley for helpfully discussing it with him.

83

Notes

[1] For a general survey of the architecture of the period, see J. Bony, *The English Decorated Style: Gothic Architecture Transformed 1250-1350* (Oxford, 1979).

[2] Howard Colvin has aptly described this programme as a 'monumental display more elaborate than that accorded to any English king or queen before or since'. (H. M. Colvin in R. A. Brown, H. M. Colvin and A. J. Taylor, *The History of the King's Works*, 1 (London, 1963), p.479.)

[3] E. M. Hallam, 'Royal Burial and the Cult of Kingship in France and England, 1060-1330', *Journal of Medieval History*, 8 (1982), pp.364-6. J.T. Rosenthal, *The Purchase of Paradise: Gift Giving and the Aristocracy, 1307-1485* (London, 1972). C. A. Bradford, *Heart Burial* (London, 1933).

[4] *King's Works*, 1, pp. 130ff.; C. Wilson, 'The Gothic Abbey Church', in C. Wilson, R. Gem, P. Tudor-Craig and J. Physick, *Westminster Abbey* (London, 1986), pp.22-69. For the French background, see also R. Branner, 'Westminster Abbey and the French Court Style', *Journal of the Society of Architectural Historians*, 23 (1964), pp.3-18 and *idem*, *St. Louis and the Court Style* (London, 1965).

[5] *King's Works*, 1, 147ff.; P. Binski, 'The Cosmati at Westminster and the English Court Style', *Art Bulletin*, 72 (1990), pp.6-34, argues for a *c.*1279 date for the shrine-base, revising P. C. Claussen, *Magistri doctissimi Romani: die römischen Marmorkünstler des Mittelalters*, Corpus Cosmatorum, 1 (Stuttgart, 1987), pp.178ff. See also J. G. O'Neilly and L. Tanner, 'The Shrine of St. Edward the Confessor', *Archaeologia*, 100 (1966), pp.129-154.

[6] W. Sauerländer, *Gothic Sculpture in France 1140-1270* (London, 1972), pp.490-1; G. R. S. Wright, 'A Royal Tomb Program in the Reign of St. Louis', *Art Bulletin*, 56 (1974), pp.224-43; A. Erlande-Brandenburg, *Le Roi est mort: Etude sur les funérailles, les sépultures et les tombeaux des rois de France jusqu' à la fin du xiiie siècle* (Geneva, 1975), pp.81-3 and 128-9; *idem.*, *L'église abbatiale de Saint-Denis: les tombeaux royaux* (Paris, 1979); A. Martindale, *Heroes, Ancestors, Relatives and the Birth of the Portrait* (Maarssen, 1988).

[7] E. A. Brown, 'The Chapel of St. Louis at Saint-denis', *Gesta*, 17 (1976), p.76. For a note of caution as to Henry III's intentions of founding a royal mausoleum in the abbey church, see S. H. Wander, 'Westminster Abbey: a case study in the meaning of medieval architecture' (unpublished PhD thesis, Stanford, 1975), pp.29-33.

[8] W. R. Lethaby, *Westminster Abbey and the Kings' Craftsmen* (London, 1906), p.284, mistakenly thought that there was a third such effigy of the queen at Blackfriars (as William Burges appears to have done, in G. G. Scott, *Gleanings from Westminster Abbey* (London, 1863), p.154), an error in which he is followed by Tudor-Craig in Wilson *et al.*, *Westminster Abbey*, p.121. It is possible that this mistake originates in B. Botfield, *Manners and Household Expenses of England in the Thirteenth and Fifteenth centuries*, ed. T. H. Turner, Roxburghe Club (1841), p.122: 'Item in cccc. et di. et i. quarterio et iij. lib. cerae, emptis pro imaginibus supra viscera Reginae apud Lincolniam et apud fratres Praedicatores Londoniae, £ix xviijs ixd, pretii c., liij.s.' and p.125, 'Item Alexandro Imaginatori et Dymenge de Legery, in partem solutionis

pro cera, pro imaginibus apud fratres Praedicatores Londoniae et Lincolniae faciendis v (marc)'. See also below, note 11.

9 For the effigies, see Colvin, *King's Works*, 1, pp.481ff.; L. Stone, *Sculpture in Britain: the Middle Ages* (Harmondsworth, 1972), pp.142-3; P. G. Lindley, '"Una grande opera al mio Re": gilt-bronze effigies in England from the Middle Ages to the Renaissance', *Journal of the British Archaeological Association*, **143** (1990), forthcoming.

10 Colvin, *King's Works*, 1, p.479.

11 Botfield, *Manners and Household Expenses*, pp.98, 100, 102-3, 108-9, 111, 113, 120, 125, 128, 131 (interestingly, the references to the three small metal images assign them to both London and Lincoln, suggesting that they may have been divided between the two monuments). Burges in Scott, *Gleanings*, p.151, note h; *King's Works*, 1, p.482. Lethaby, *Craftsmen*, p.297 notes that Adam had in 1284 been employed in making the pinnacles of the gold shrine of St. Thomas at Canterbury. See also Botfield, *Manners and Household Expenses*, pp.lxxvi-lxxvii. Bony, *Decorated Style*, p.20, has conjectured that the heart-tomb looked something like that of Count Thibaut's heart memorial at Provins (plate 117). For the location of Eleanor's heart-tomb, see W. A. Hinnebusch, *The Early English Friars Preachers* (Rome, 1951), p.45; the assumption that this chapel was in the north aisle of the choir would reconcile Walsingham's statement that the heart was buried in the choir of the church with the payment in 1292 to Friar Robert of Newmarket for the adornment of the 'chapel of the Friars Preachers where the queen's heart lies'. The church, which was unique among English Dominican houses in having an aisled choir, was destroyed by Sir Thomas Cawarden after 1550 (W. Martin and S. Toy, 'The Black Friars in London: A Chapter in National History', *Transactions of the London and Middlesex Archaeological Society*, NS 5 (1929), pp.353-79). Queen Eleanor gave £100 in February 1290 to build her chapel: see J. C. Parsons, *The Court and Household of Eleanor of Castile* (Toronto, 1977), pp.17, 24, 88.

12 Sauerländer, *Sculpture*, p.467, pl.174, ill. 188; N. Rogers, 'English Episcopal Monuments, 1270-1350', in J. Coales (ed.), *The Earliest English Brasses* (London, 1987), pp.8-68 (21); see also S. Badham, 'A Lost Bronze Effigy of 1279 from York Minster', *Antiquarian Journal*, **60** (1980), pp.59-65.

13 Colvin, *King's Works*, 1, pp.478-9, and J. D. Tanner, 'The Tombs of the Royal Babies in Westminster Abbey', *Journal of the British Archaeological Association*, **16** (1953), pp.25-40. Cf. Louis IX's tombs for his infant daughter Blanche (d.1243) and baby son Jean (d.1248).

14 *Calendar of Liberate Rolls*, 4 (1251-60), pp.376, 385, 448; Colvin, *King's Works*, 1, p.478, and Tanner, 'Royal Babies', citing PRO Issue Roll 41 Henry III, m.5, have 80 marks, whereas the published account has 50.

15 *Calendar of Liberate Rolls*, 4 (1251-60), pp.376, 385; Scott, *Gleanings*, p.113; Colvin, *King's Works*, 1, p.478. Tanner, 'Royal Babies', p.27 believed this to have been a 'statue', which 'probably represented St. Katherine' rather than a tomb effigy as is surely much more likely. Perhaps she derived the idea from William Burges's account, in Scott, *Gleanings*, p.146, where he conjectures that 'the silver image

represented St. Catherine, while the bronze one might be a kneeling figure of the princess'.

16 This point is made in the account of Katherine's tomb given in Colvin, *King's Works*, 1, p.478. For the Limoges effigy, see W. R. Lethaby, *Westminster Abbey Re-examined* (London, 1925), pp.278-80; Stone, *Sculpture*, p.135.

17 H. J. Plenderleith and H. Maryon, 'The Royal Bronze Effigies in Westminster Abbey', *Antiquaries' Journal*, 39 (1959), p.87.

18 E403/70, Issue Roll Michaelmas 19 Edward I, cited in *King's Works*, 1, p.481, n.3, 'Hugoni de Kendale super factura cuiusdam domus in cimiterio abbacie westm' in qua ymagines R. Henrici et Alianore Regine Anglie dudum consortis Regis nunc parantur faciend'.

19 Botfield, *Manners and Household Expenses*, pp.98, 122, 125, 128.

20. Botfield, *Manners and Household Expenses*, pp.95, 100, 117-8, 132; *Calendar of the Close Rolls*, 3, 1288-96 (London, 1904), p.171; Lethaby, *Craftsmen*, p.284.

21 For the date of completion, see Colvin, *King's Works*, 1, p.481.

22 Conveniently accessible in J. J. G. Alexander and P. Binski (eds.) *Age of Chivalry: Art in Plantagenet England 1200-1400* (London, 1987), p.366 (British Library, Loan MS 38, ff 98ᵛ-99ʳ). If this depiction is reasonably accurate, the tomb-chest differed from that at Westminster in having fewer panels each side and in the form of the pinnacles.

23 *Manners and Household Expenses*, pp.122-3, 124-5, 131, 135. For the grille see Royal Commission on Historical Monuments, *Westminster Abbey* (London, 1924), pp.29-30, plates 50-52 and for its cost, *Manners and Household Expenses*, p.131.

24 Lethaby, *Craftsmen*, p.177.

25 Lethaby, *Craftsmen*, pp.262-3 (and, for his later view, 'Medieval Paintings at Westminster', *Proceedings of the British Academy*, 13 (1927), pp.140-2). For the style, see P. Binski, *The Painted Chamber at Westminster* (London, 1986), pp.78-9. The analysis of the tomb offered by Binski, 'Cosmati', p.6, contrasts its 'representational understatement, a reduction of the tomb's imagery to a depersonalized imagery of official attributes... and a rejection of... applied polychromy', with the tombs of the royal circle. Quite apart from the fact that Eleanor's tomb almost certainly *predates* those of Aveline and Crouchback with which he compares it (so that, if anything, they must be rejecting *its* characteristics), there is the point that with its tester and basement paintings and possible tile pavement, the tomb certainly featured a good deal of imagery. It could be more convincingly argued that it stands at the beginning of the evolution of rich multi-media funerary imagery at Westminster, a development which the less costly and later tombs of Aveline and Crouchback help expand. For the tiles, see E. C. Norton, 'The British Museum Collection of Medieval Tiles', *Journal of the British Archaeological Association*, 124 (1981), pp.111-112. Nothing in the architectural vocabulary of the tiles rules out a date in the mid-1290s but the identification of Queen Eleanor is uncertain. The queen is, very probably, also depicted in the glass of the vestibule to York Minster chapter house, as Norton notes.

[26] Plenderleith and Maryon, 'Effigies', pp.87-90. The beast(s) at Henry's feet were cast separately and have been stolen: Keepe records a lion at the feet and the existence of the canopy above Henry's head in 1681 (J. P. Neale, *The History and Antiquities of Westminster Abbey* (London, 1856), p.33).

[27] Presumably these were not unlike the paste jewels discovered in 1774 on the stole in which Edward I had been buried in 1307 (see Neale, *Westminster*, p.31, note 5). The gilding of the tomb-chest mouldings, the appearance of the fictive gems, the painted tester and tomb-basement, the figurative tiles and the painting of the grille, suggest that the dichotomy seen by Binski, 'Cosmati', pp.6-7, between the 'restrained display of pure polychromy, pure materials' of the royal monuments on the one hand, and the 'applied not structural polychromy...[the] preference for multiplicity of technique and detailed effect' of the near-contemporary ones of the royal circle on the other hand (revealingly, the monument of William de Valence is left out of this analysis), may be a little overdrawn. It seems to me likely that the relative costs of these monuments explain their differences more satisfactorily than supposing that contrasting aesthetic tastes lie behind them.

[28] Lethaby, *Craftsmen*, p.287; Colvin, *King's Works*, 1, p.482; Stone, *Sculpture*, p.143.

[29] Architectural niches for tomb-sculptures are commonly found from the late twelfth century onwards. See E. S. Prior and A. Gardner, *An Account of Medieval Figure-Sculpture in England* (Cambridge, 1912), pp.573ff; Stone, *Sculpture*, p.143.

[30] See E. Panofsky, *Tomb Sculpture* (London, 1964), pp.54ff.

[31] J. Armitage Robinson, 'Effigies of Saxon Bishops at Wells', *Archaeologia*, **65** (1914), pp.95-112.

[32] For this issue, see Martindale, *Heroes*.

[33] Compare the extraordinary thirteenth-century lady and child at Scarcliffe in Derbyshire, which reproduces the Madonna and Child format in a tomb-sculpture (A. Gardner, *English Medieval Sculpture* (Cambridge, 1951), fig. 407).

[34] J. H. Harvey, *English Medieval Architects* (Gloucester, 1984), sub Robert of Beverley, takes up Lethaby's (*Craftsmen*, p.170) suggestion that Torel's effigy was cast from a wax funeral effigy of Henry III. There is, however, no clear evidence for the existence of such an effigy. I am discussing the Westminster funeral effigies in a volume edited by R. Mortimer and A. Harvey (Boydell and Brewer, forthcoming).

[35] Eg., Stone, *Sculpture*, p.143, derives the 'high forehead, the shape of the crown, the thick neck and firm chin [and] and the slight sway of the figure' from the painting of St. Faith, which is more convincingly dated to the late thirteenth or early fourteenth century by Binski, *Painted Chamber*, p.80, and which is anyway of limited usefulness as a comparison with the bronze effigy.

[36] Compare Stone, *Sculpture*, plate 111A.

[37] Stone, *Sculpture*, p.143. Compare P. Tudor-Craig, *One Half of our Noblest Art* (Wells, 1976), fig. 10 (183). It is impossible to agree with Stone, *Sculpture*, p.143, that the 'full modelling of the figure...and the sinuous rippling of the edges of the

cloak, are both features of effigies of thirty years before, for example that of Archbishop de Gray at York'. A comparison of the effigies (for de Gray, see Prior and Gardner, *Account*, fig. 661, or H. G. Ramm *et al.*, 'The Tombs of Archbishops Walter de Gray (1216-55) and Godfrey de Ludham (1258-65), in York Minster, and their contents', *Archaeologia*, **103** (1971), pp.100-147, plate xxxvii), merely highlights the fact that the long pleats of Eleanor's draperies, the subtle manner in which the line of the cloak accentuates the *déhanchement* of the pose and the elegance of the modelling are without precedent in the Purbeck marble effigy of the archbishop.

[38] Stone, *Sculpture*, chapter 10.

[39] Cf. RCHM, *Westminster*, p.29 and plate 185.

[40] The brooch should be compared with the central element of the patera from the ceiling of the Painted Chamber at Westminster, Binski *Painted Chamber*, pl. xxxiii; (where the patera has unfortunately been turned at 45°).

[41] Compare Gardner, *English Medieval Sculpture*, figs. 359 and 424.

[42] Stone, *Sculpture*, p.143 makes a very similar comment on Eleanor's effigy but pays surprisingly little attention to Henry III's figure.

[43] An introduction to the vast literature on the Eleanor crosses is provided by W. Lovell, 'Queen Eleanor's Crosses', *Archaeological Journal*, **49** (1892), pp.17-43; Colvin, *King's Works*, 1, pp.483-485, and Bony, *Decorated Style, passim*; *The Age of Chivalry*, pp.361-4. For the montjoies, see R. Branner, 'The Montjoies of Saint Louis', in D. Fraser, H. Hibbard and M. J. Lewine (eds.), *Essays in the History of Architecture presented to R. Wittkower* (London, 1967), pp.13-16.

[44] See also C. Wilson, 'The origins of the Perpendicular Style and its Development to *c.*1360', unpublished PhD thesis, University of London, 1980, chapter 2. Five crosses - St. Albans, Dunstable, Stony Stratford, Woburn and Northampton (Hardingstone) - were put into the hands of a single master mason, John of Battle, and the important cross at Cheapside was contracted to Michael of Canterbury, for £300. See Harvey, *English Medieval Architects*, sub Michael of Canterbury. Two fragments of the Cheapside cross survive in the Museum of London.

[45] Lethaby, *Westminster Abbey Re-examined*, pp.197-9; Harvey, *English Medieval Architects*, sub Alexander of Abingdon; P. Williamson, *Northern Gothic Sculpture 1200-1540* (Victoria and Albert Museum, 1988), pp.63-5 (entry by Peta Evelyn). The accounts do not specify that Alexander sculpted these images but show that he provided ten images and that he worked on the Waltham and Charing crosses (that he provided images for the latter *is* detailed). It is virtually certain, therefore, that he carved the Waltham figures. For Alexander, see also M. J. H. Liversidge, 'Alexander of Abingdon', in W. J. H. and M. J. H. Liversidge, *Abingdon Essays: Studies in Local History* (Abingdon, 1989), pp.89-111. Liversidge notes that Alexander is always referred to as a sculptor and infers from this that he was not a mason carver of the artisan type but a specialist in figure work.

[46] I am grateful to Paul Williamson, Curator of Sculpture and John Larson, Head of the Sculpture Conservation Section of the Victoria and Albert Museum, for permission to study this figure, and to the former for the two record photographs of the other images, one of which has a nineteenth-century head, evidently that carved by Sir

Richard Westmacott in 1833 (see W. Winters, *The Queen Eleanor Memorial, Waltham Cross* (Waltham Abbey, 1885), p.39). I was able briefly to see the figures in their packing crates in January 1984.

[47] Harvey, *English Medieval Architects*, sub Crundale: cf. Wilson, 'Origins', chapter 2; Colvin, *King's Works*, 1, p.483; Botfield, *Manners and Household Expenses*, p.124, for Alexander's Charing images.

[48] *Age of Chivalry*, p.364.

[49] Binski, *Painted Chamber*, compares the figure-style of the Crouchback tomb weepers with the Madonna Master's work. See L. F. Sandler, *The De Lisle Psalter in the British Library* (Oxford, 1983).

[50] Stone, *Sculpture*, p.147.

[51] Stone, *Sculpture*, pp.146-7, distinguishes different styles in the Crouchback weepers.

[52] Prior and Gardner, *Account*, fig.395, right hand image. The front of the draperies, down to the knee, is completely lost, and may have been handled differently. The third image, that with a replacement head, appears to have had a series of v-shaped folds across the front of the body (the head of the second image, to judge from my own photograph, taken in 1984, appears to be in better condition than that of the image currently undergoing conservation).

[53] Botfield, *Manners and Household Expenses*, pp.125, 128, 131. It is not absolutely clear from these entries whether one or more of these three small images may have been intended for Lincoln; one entry has in the margin 'imagines pro corde et pro visceribus' whilst another reads, '*Imagines*, Videlicet, Willielmo de Suffolke, in perpacationem pro factura imaginum de metallo, pro Regina, apud fratres Praedicatores et apud Lincolniam. 4 marc'.

[54] The conservation work on the sculptures was carried out by Messrs Harrison and Hill, of Little Oakley, Northamptonshire, to whom I am indebted for the opportunity of studying the figures during conservation.

[55] Stone, *Sculpture*, p.144. For William of Ireland, see Harvey, *English Medieval Architects*, sub Ireland. William was paid for five images, the fifth figure going to an unspecified cross (possibly that at Lincoln, for which he worked other sculptural details: Botfield, *Manners and Household Expenses*, p.123).

[56] Stone, *Sculpture*, p.144 (though he admits that William's workshop was in London).

[57] Botfield, *Manners and Household Expenses*, p.127. For the debate on the court style, see, most recently, H. M. Colvin, 'The "Court Style" in Medieval English Architecture: a review', in V. J. Scattergood and J. W. Sherborne, *English Court Culture in the Later Middle Ages* (London, 1983), pp.129-139, and Binski, *Painted Chamber*, pp.105-112.

[58] Two images of the Waltham cross appear in Prior and Gardner, *Account*, fig. 395, and one of the Hardingstone queens (fig. 387; a general view appears in fig. 90); Gardner, *Sculpture*, figs. 318 and 319, uses the same photographs, selecting the best preserved Waltham image to contrast with that at Hardingstone. The latter image is again reproduced by Stone, *Sculpture*, plate 109(B) (he does not illustrate the Waltham

89

queens). I recall the third of the Waltham queens as having a rather different drapery treatment from the other two figures, with v-shaped folds over the stomach.

⁵⁹ Botfield, *Manners and Household Expenses*, p.134.

⁶⁰ In addition to the literature cited in note 43, above, see W. H. A. Vallance, *Old Crosses and Lych-gates* (London, 1920), pp.94-108; Evans, 'A Prototype of the Eleanor Crosses', pp.96-99; J. Evans, 'Geddington Cross', *Archaeological Journal*, **110** (1953), p.200; J. Zukowsky, 'Montjoies and Eleanor Crosses Reconsidered', *Gesta*, **13** (1974), pp.39-44 (figure 2, from the Luttrell Psalter, is of importance in suggesting the original termination, with an image of the crucified Christ, of the crosses; this would have been an obvious target for iconoclasts. Such terminations, which are recorded in the accounts as being of marble, would also explain why sculptors were required to carve these details). As has been noted, most recently by Liversidge, 'Alexander', p.92, the fact that the Geddington cross does not appear in the extant accounts, which cover the period 1291-4, implies that it was constructed between 1294 and 1297. Liversidge suggests, p.100, that its different character from the larger and more ornate crosses at Hardingstone and Waltham may have been due to a shortage of money.

⁶¹ There is a clear change of stone close to the top of the lower stage.

⁶² N. Smith, 'The Eleanor Cross, Geddington', *Conservation Bulletin* (June 1988), pp.8-10, below pp.94-96. In connection with the extraordinary masking of the image by the buttress, the point might be made that in the exterior elevation of St. Stephen's Chapel, the lower chapel windows were also masked by the descending mullions of the grid-like surface treatment. Was this the source for the Geddington designer?

⁶³ See P. Williamson's essay in *Age of Chivalry*, pp.98-106.

⁶⁴ L. F. Salzman, *Building in England down to 1540* (London, 1967), p.31.

⁶⁵ *Gleanings*, p.41. For these figures, see Stone, *Sculpture*, pp.120-1; S. E. Rigold, *The Chapter House and the Pyx Chamber* (HMSO, 1976), pp.18-22; P. Tudor-Craig, in *Age of Chivalry*, pp.319-320 (doubting the attribution to Yxeworth); P. Williamson, 'The Westminster Abbey Chapter House Annunciation Group', *Burlington Magazine*, **130** (1988), pp.122-4; *idem*, 'The Westminster Abbey Chapter House "Annunciation" Group', *Burlington Magazine*, **130** (1988), p.928. The different iconography and stones (the Virgin is of Reigate, the Angel of Caen stone) from which they are carved (and hence the differences in the deterioration) explain a great deal of the differences in style which Dr. Tudor-Craig has seen between the two figures (P. Tudor-Craig in Wilson *et al.*, *Westminster Abbey*, p.96). Different stones were regularly used within sculptural programmes at Westminster: cf. C. J. P. Cave, 'A Thirteenth-Century Choir of Angels in the North Transept of Westminster Abbey and the Adjacent Figures of Two Kings', *Archaeologia*, **84** (1935), pp.63-67.

⁶⁶ There is a vast body of literature on the thirteenth-century sculpture at Westminster Abbey: amongst the more important studies additional to those mentioned in the notes above, see J. G. Noppen, 'Sculpture of the School of John of St. Albans', *Burlington Magazine*, **51** (1927), pp.79-80; 'Further Sculptures of the Westminster School', *Burlington Magazine*, **53** (1928), 74; 'Recently Cleaned Sculptures at Westminster', *Burlington Magazine*, **58** (1930), pp.139-40; R. P. Howgrave-Graham, 'Westminster

Abbey: Various Bosses, Capitals and Corbels of the Thirteenth Century', *Journal of the British Archaeological Association*, ser. 3, **8** (1943), pp.1-4; 'Westminster Abbey. The Sequence and Dates of the Transepts and Nave', *Journal of the British Archaeological Association*, ser. 3, **11** (1948), pp.60-78; L. Tanner, *Unknown Westminster Abbey* (Harmondsworth, 1948); D. Carpenter, 'Westminster Abbey: Some Characteristics of its Sculpture 1245-59', *Journal of the British Archaeological Association*, ser. 3, **35** (1972), pp.1-14; Wander, 'Westminster Abbey, A Case Study in the Meaning of Medieval Architecture'. A good guide to the literature is found in Colvin, *King's Works*, 1, pp.130-157.

[67] For the Judgement Portal at Lincoln, see W. R. Lethaby, 'Notes on Sculptures in Lincoln Minster: the Judgement Porch and the Angel Choir', *Archaeologia*, **60** (1907), pp.379-90; Stone, *Sculpture*, pp. 125-7, 130-1. For the connection with Westminster, see also M. E. Roberts, 'The Relic of the Holy Blood and the Iconography of the Thirteenth-Century North Transept Portal of Westminster Abbey', in W. M. Ormrod (ed.), *England in the Thirteenth Century* (Grantham, 1985), pp.129-142. For the Angel Choir sculpture, see C. J. P. Cave, *Lincoln Roof [sic] Bosses*, Lincoln Minster Pamphlet 3 (3rd edition, 1973); A. Gardner, *Lincoln Angels*, Lincoln Minster Pamphlet 4 (2nd edition, n.d.); V. Glenn, 'The Sculpture of the Angel Choir at Lincoln', in *Medieval Art and Architecture at Lincoln Cathedral*, British Archaeological Association Conference Transactions, **8** (1982), pp.102-8. For a recent study of the iconography, see T. A. Heslop, 'The Iconography of the Angel Choir', in E. Fernie and P. Crossley (eds.), *Medieval Architecture and its Intellectual Context: Studies in Honour of Peter Kidson* (London, 1990), pp.151-8 (interestingly omitting to consider the north aisle bosses).

[68] Stone, *Sculpture*, pp.130-131.

[69] L. L. Gee, '"Ciborium" Tombs in England, 1290-1330', *Journal of the British Archaeological Association*, **132** (1979), pp.29-41.

[70] For G. G. Scott's reconstruction of exactly this type of decoration, which can be compared with the unrestored remnants, see the closest imitator of Crouchback's tomb, at Ely: P. G. Lindley, 'The Tomb of Bishop William de Luda: an Architectural Model at Ely Cathedral', *Proceedings of the Cambridge Antiquarian Society*, **73** (1984), pp.75-87 (cf. Scott's treatment of this monument with his plans for Philippa of Hainault's tomb). For the figures painted on the basement of Crouchback's monument, see Lethaby, *Craftsmen*, pp.269-71: they are very close in style to the Old Testament scenes of the Painted Chamber (compare Binski, *Painted Chamber*, plate xxiv).

[71] Wilson, 'Origins', chapter 1.

[72] Stone, *Sculpture*, pp.145-6.

[73] As indeed they are on the south and east sides of Eleanor's tomb-chest (see illustration 9). Wilson, 'Origins', pp.33-4, was the first to comment on this change.

[74] W. H. St. J. Hope, 'The Obituary Roll of John Islip, Abbot of Westminster, 1500-1532', *Vetusta Monumenta*, **7**, part iv (1906).

[75] Stone, *Sculpture*, p.160, brilliantly employs the horsemen of the canopy spandrels to highlight the differences between Crouchback's and William de Valence's (d.1324) tombs: the Crouchback relief has an elegant solemnity and is set against a painted

91

textured surface. The Valence horseman, on the other hand, is "set against a carved diaper background, and the horse's feet are perched precariously on two isolated tufts of rock as he gallops" across the space. "The sense of unreality" is "enhanced by the mantling of the helmet" which flies out both backwards and forwards.

[76] Prior and Gardner, *Account*, figs. 389 and 730; Stone, *Sculpture*, pp.145-6.

[77] Stone, *Sculpture*, p.146; H. A. Tummers, *Early Secular Effigies in England: The Thirteenth Century* (Leiden, 1980), pp.29-30; *idem*, 'The Medieval Effigial Tombs in Chichester Cathedral', *Church Monuments*, 3 (1988), 26-31.

[78] Stone, *Sculpture*, p.146.

[79] Stone, *Sculpture*, pp.146-7.

[80] This would place the date of the monument in the mid-1290s, after the cross images and tombs of Queen Eleanor, but before Crouchback's tomb, a dating which would fit well with modern studies (e.g. Gee, 'Tombs', p.33).

[81] See Lindley, 'Una grande opera' (forthcoming; see note 9).

[82] These developments deserve further study, see Stone, *Sculpture*, chapter 12.

[83] William, for instance, is also described as a *cementarius* which may just imply his working on decorative as well as figurative sculpture. It may mean, however, that he also worked as a mason. Possibly, outside major cities such as London, sculptors would generally undertake a very wide range of work, including non-sculptural stonework.

[84] For the *Opus*, see Professor Parsons's essay in this volume. Professor Parsons suggests to me that there is a depiction of Queen Eleanor in the Alphonso Psalter (British Library, MS Additional 24686), for which see L. F. Sandler, *Gothic Manuscripts 1285-1385*, 2 (Oxford, 1986), I. This essay was written in eleven days, in order for it to appear in time for the 700th anniversary of Queen Eleanor's death and there was no time for me to see the manuscript.

[85] *Annales Monastici*, 3, ed. H. R. Luard, Rolls Series (London, 1866), pp.362-3.

[86] *Willelmi Rishanger, Quondam Monachi S. Albani, et Quorundam Anonymorum, Chronica et Annales*, ed. H. T. Riley, Rolls Series (London, 1865), p.121.

[87] Lovell, 'Crosses', pp.19-24; Branner, 'Montjoies', p.14. J. Evans, 'A Prototype of the Eleanor Crosses', *Burlington Magazine*, 91 (1949), p.99, suggests that the Eleanor crosses may also have been intended as a prelude to canonisation, but I know of no evidence to support this conjecture.

[88] For an alternative view, see Binski, *Painted Chamber*, p.111.

[89] For Edward's use of romance, *ibid.*, and M. Prestwich, *The Three Edwards* (London, 1980), pp.35-7. On his death, Edward I had wished his body to be borne with the army until the Scots had been defeated, whilst his heart was to be borne to the Holy Land accompanied by one hundred knights. These desires graphically illustrate the intersection of a romance-influenced chivalry with his political and religious attitudes. (Neither wish was fulfilled by Edward II.)

APPENDIX

A Note on the Conservation of the Geddington Cross

Dr. Nicola Smith

The Eleanor Cross in Geddington, Northamptonshire, which has recently been conserved on behalf of English Heritage, is the most complete survivor of the twelve crosses erected by Edward I in memory of his queen, Eleanor of Castile. Crosses were erected at Lincoln, Grantham, Stamford, Geddington, Northampton, Stony Stratford, Woburn, Dunstable, St Albans, Waltham, West Cheap, and Charing, but only those at Geddington, Northampton, and Waltham survive. In the seventeenth century, Protestant zeal hastened the removal of several of them. Charing Cross, for example, was demolished in 1647 by order of Parliament.

> The Committee said, that verily
> To popery it was bent;
> For ought I know, it might be so,
> For to church it never went

commented a wry contemporary ballad lamenting its loss.

In the early eighteenth century, however, when a number of antiquaries began to take an interest in preserving Gothic monuments, steps were taken to repair and protect the remaining Eleanor Crosses. The first recorded repair of the Northampton cross took place in 1713, and in 1720 the newly-founded Society of Antiquaries of London arranged for posts to be put up to protect Waltham Cross from damage by carts. Minor patchwork repairs and restoration were carried out on both crosses later in the eighteenth century.

As the nineteenth century advanced and interest in all things medieval became a general fashion, the Eleanor Crosses became the subject of sentimental attachment and the model for many Victorian monuments. Of these, the Martyrs' Memorial in Oxford, based on Waltham Cross, is probably the most archaeologically correct, but there are many others more loosely based on the same examples. Even the Albert Memorial was intended to echo them, as its architect, George Gilbert Scott, explained: 'I have not hesitated to adopt in my design the style at once most congenial with my own feelings, and that of the most touching monuments ever erected in this country to a Royal Consort - the exquisite "Eleanor Crosses"'. The present Charing Cross, an advertising ploy on the part of the Charing Cross Hotel Company, dates from 1864.

It might be said that the crosses at Waltham and Northampton suffered from an excess of attention from this time, since the former has twice been rebuilt and although the latter has not undergone such wholesale remodelling, it has been worked on many times and now incorporates a good deal of replaced stonework.

Geddington Cross, on the other hand, survived virtually unscathed under the watchful eyes of successive Dukes of Buccleuch from nearby Boughton House, who took responsibility for its upkeep until 1915 when it passed into the care of the state. Only the steps around it had been replaced and the sound and secure condition of the original fabric was remarked upon. The honey-coloured, open-structured, and fossiliferous local limestone had proved remarkably durable.

In the winter of 1927-8 Geddington Cross was repointed, all the exposed iron cramps and dowels were replaced with Delta metal, and a missing finial was replaced in new stone. Thereafter no major work was considered necessary until recently, when the limestone, especially at the higher levels, had begun to laminate and decay, and the cross had become masked by lichen growth and sulphation. A programme of conservation was planned by experts from English Heritage and the work was carried out by Harrison Hill Limited between June and August 1987.

The overriding aim was to extend the life of the original fabric and no stone was replaced. Repointing, where necessary, was carried out using a mortar mix consisting of one part HTI powder, three parts lime, and six parts crushed stone to replace bedding material, and a stronger mix of one part HTI, one part lime, and three parts crushed stone for the final surface pointing. Cleaning of the architectural framework, carried out inch by inch with scalpels and brushes, revealed the banding of the stonework where a darker, harder limestone had been used in the construction of the most exposed areas at the top of the base shaft and above the canopies.

The gables of the canopies had suffered considerable decay. Eltoline tissue and polyvinyl alcohol were used to support the delicate exfoliating areas here before any work could be attempted. Loose debris was removed from behind the supported detail, and then mortar was carefully built up to fill the voids. Lichen and other deposits could then be removed to allow further fine surface pointing around the supported detail. Especially vulnerable areas, such as the finials, were capped with mortar, and a mortar weathering was built up behind the pinnacles. The Delta metal ties were left in place, but an iron dowel which had fractured the south-west finial was replaced with stainless steel; this and the damaged stonework around it were fixed with a polyester adhesive.

The figures, which are of a finely grained, possibly French, limestone, were found to be in a sound condition despite the inevitable overall loss of surface. The heavy sulphation to the faces was not removed because most of the fine carved detail was found to be preserved only in the sulphate skin. The sulphate deposits to the underside of the canopies were also left in case any traces of original paint might survive in these sheltered areas, for it is likely that the monument was originally painted. Traces of paint have recently been discovered on the original statues from the Waltham Cross which are now in the Victoria and Albert Museum.

The treatment which the cross at Geddington has recently received has been as delicate and as painstaking as if it were an object in a museum. Monuments in the care of English Heritage are almost by definition both of exceptional importance and incapable of beneficial use. In building terms they are the equivalent of objects taken into the national museum collections and as such they deserve equivalent treatment. At Geddington in 1987 we had an opportunity to put the best ideals of current conservation theory into practice.

*The substance of this note first appeared in the **Conservation Bulletin** for June 1988, pp.8-10. It is reprinted here with the permission of HBMC.*

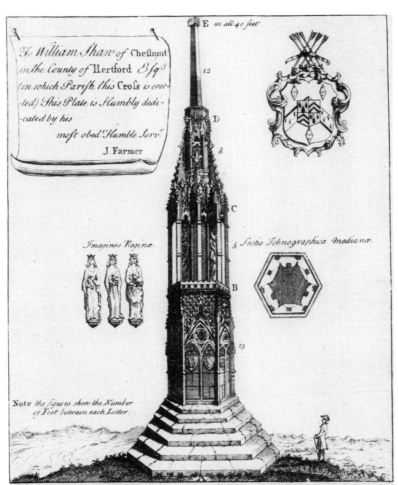

E _in all 40 feet_

To William Shaw of Cheshunt
in the County of Hertford _Esq.
(in which Parish this_ Cross _is erected) This Plate is Humbly dedi-
-cated by his
most obed.t Humble Serv.t_
J. Farmer

12

D

8

C

Imagines Reginæ.

5 Sectio Ichnographica media næ.

B

15

Note _the figures shew the Number of Feet between each Letter._

This Cross erected by King Edward the first in the year 1290 takes Name from ye Vicinity of our Town and the then Famous Abby of Waltham, _and was in Memory of Prou. Dr. Eleanor the Beloved Wife of that Glorious Monarch, who accompanied Him into the Holy Land, where her Royal Husband being stabbed with a poisoned Dagger by a Sarazen, and the Rank Wound judged incurable by his Physicians. She full of Love, Care, and Affection, adventur'd Her own Life to save his by sucking out the Substance of the Poison, that the Wounds being Closed and Cicatrized he became perfectly healed. She was the only Daughter of Ferdinando the Third, King of_ Castile _and_ Leon, _and Died at_ Hardeby _near the Citty of_ Lincoln 29.th _November 1290 having been King Edward's Wife 36 years, Who erected in Honour of Her those Crosses as Statues where Her Body rested, viz at_ Lincoln, Grantham, Stamford, Giddington, Northampton, Stony-Stratford, Dunstable _(now destroyed)_ St. Albans _and this at_ Waltham _(being the most Curious in Workmanship)_ Tottenham _&_ Westminster _called_ Chairing Cross, _all adorned with the Arms of_ Castile _and_ Leon _and the Earldom & County of_ Ponthieu _which by Her Right was annexed to the Crown of_ England.

2   **Waltham Cross** from J. Falmer's *The History of the Ancient Town
     and the once Famous Abbey of Waltham* (London, 1735)
     supplied by Conway Library, Courtauld Institute of Art

3　**Hardingstone Cross**
copyright Royal Commission on the Historical Monuments of
England (RCHME)

4   **Geddington Cross**
copyright Courtauld Institute of Art

5   **Westminster Abbey: tomb of Edmund Crouchback**
copyright Courtauld Institute of Art

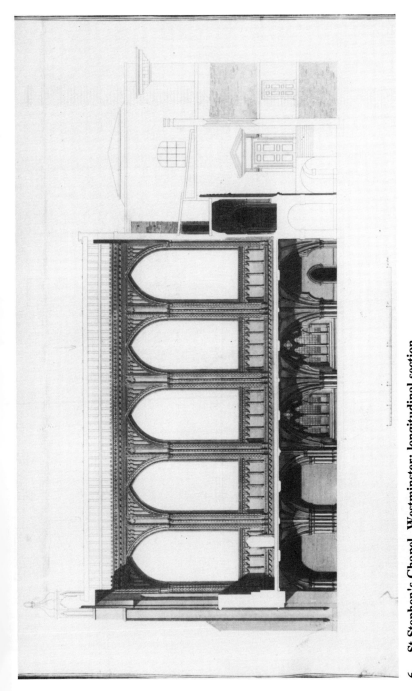

6 **St Stephen's Chapel, Westminster: longitudinal section**
copyright Courtauld Institute of Art

7   **Westminster Abbey: interior of choir**
copyright RCHME

8 **St Etheldreda's, Holborn: interior**
copyright Courtauld Institute of Art

NOTE. The dotted lines at A. indicate the principal lines of the frame of an elaborate piece of ironwork.

¾ inch Scale

NOTE. The S.W. side & S.E. end have no shafts but the mouldings run down and return at the bottom as shown at B.

Plan at the Angle. ½ full size.

Mullion. ½ full size.

Tracery Mouldings. ½ full size.

The at (The the the (

B.

C.

D.

W. DAVIE.

9 **Westminster Abbey: Queen Eleanor's tomb**
Drawing from Architectural Association Sketch Book, 1867-8

QVEEN·ELEANOR·

NOTE. The Metal Figure and Canopy are not taken from measurements.

1/8 th full size

Top Mouldings 1/4 full size

Base Mouldings 1/4 full size

HALF FULL SIZE

10   Westminster Abbey: head of tomb effigy of Queen Eleanor
copyright RCHME

11   Westminster Abbey: tomb effigy of Queen Eleanor (ex situ), photograph Helmut Gernsheim, 1943, supplied by RCHME

12   **Westminster Abbey: head of tomb effigy of King Henry III**
copyright RCHME

13

Hardingstone Cross: Queen Eleanor statue
copyright RCHME

16 **Waltham cross: image**
photograph by courtesy of the Victoria
and Albert Museum

17 **Geddington Cross: image**
copyright P. G. Lindley

18　**Geddington Cross: image head**
copyright Harrison-Hill